D0507149

CREATING INDEPENDENT STUDENT LEARNERS

A PRACTICAL GUIDE TO ASSESSMENT FOR LEARNING

Pauline Clarke, Thompson Owens, Ruth Sutton

PORTAGE & MAIN PRESS

Portage and Main Press acknowledges the financial support of the Government of Canada through the Book Publishing Industry Development Program (BPIDP) for our publishing activities.

Cover and text design: Relish Design Studio LTD.
Cover photo: iStockphoto
Printed and bound in Canada by Friesens

Library and Archives Canada Cataloguing in Publication

Clarke, Pauline, 1947-
    Creating independent student learners, school leaders : a practical guide to assessment for learning / Pauline Clarke, Thompson Owens, Ruth Sutton.

Includes bibliographical references.
ISBN 1-55379-089-8

    1. School children--Rating of. I. Owens, Thompson, 1947-
II. Sutton, Ruth, 1948- III. Title.

LB3060.22.C555 2006   372.126   C2006-904217-9

ISBN-10: 1-55379-089-8
ISBN-13: 978-1-55379-089-1

PORTAGE & MAIN PRESS

100 – 318 McDermot Ave.
Winnipeg, MB Canada R3A 0A2

Email: books@portageandmainpress.com
Tel: 204-987-3500
Toll-free: 1-800-667-9673
Toll-free fax: 1-866-734-8477

Printed on 30% PCW paper.

To all the teachers of the Winnipeg School Division Inner City who are not named in this book, but who worked diligently as we all tried to find the best ways to help our students succeed.

Acknowledgments

The authors wish to thank the Winnipeg School Division for permission to publish references to Feedback for Learning.

CONTENTS

INTRODUCTION

The Reason for This Book

This book came about as the result of a project we undertook about student assessment, which we called *Feedback for Learning*. Inner City District is one of four districts that together comprise the Winnipeg School Division in Winnipeg, Manitoba, Canada. There are 21 schools in all, of which 10 were involved most closely in the work. Most of the teachers participating in the Feedback for Learning project worked in elementary or junior high settings.

The Inner City District contains some of the most impoverished and diverse communities in Canada. The schools and teachers represent the best of the country's inner-city education programs, driven by the high needs of the students and a strong sense of urgency. The superintendent, Pauline Clarke, has led this district for 16 years: her vision, determination, expectations, and commitment to these students and their families are an essential backdrop to the work. It was she and the Inner City school leaders who brought the Feedback for Learning project into being in 2000. The district and the schools together provided the budget, recognized the skills of the support teacher – Thompson Owens – and recruited the external consultant – Ruth Sutton. Much of our experience is reflected in the present book. Practical guidance to school leaders is tempered with the recognition of the complexity of the task of school leadership. At the end of each stage in this book are Frequently Asked Questions (FAQs) and responses to them that acknowledge and address that complexity.

Feedback for Learning was based firmly on the research into assessment for learning published over the past 30 years, including the seminal global study by Paul Black and Dylan Wiliam in 1998, "Inside the Black Box: Raising Standards

Through Classroom Assessment." Our goal was to investigate the practical implications of the link among assessment, learning, and metacognition. We aimed to change teachers' classroom habits, to improve student outcomes, and to pursue sustainability.

The work, therefore, has two strands: one is the development of assessment for learning in the classroom; the other is sustainable school improvement. The three books for teachers, *Creating Independent Student Learners*, developed for different grade levels, provide practical guidance for classroom activity and professional development. This book has assessment for learning as the context, and is also about school improvement and the implications for school leaders – teachers and leaders as adult learners – and changing the way the school does business.

The Structure of the Book

Feedback for Learning in Inner City Winnipeg was a three-year project, leading to the embedding of specific approaches to teaching and leadership into the fabric of the schools. This process still continues. Three stages, roughly connected to these first three years, provide the book's structure. In Stage One, the introduction of assessment for learning is just beginning. In Stage Two, assessment is consolidated and spreads. In Stage Three, we are preparing for long-term sustainability. At the beginning of each stage is a brief foreword that describes how the work in Winnipeg Inner City was developing at that time, to connect the guidance to a specific reality, with further examples and experience, also drawn from a wider range of contexts. The work of all those involved in Winnipeg Inner City is both honoured and supplemented.

This is not a piece of research, dispassionately observed and recorded for other researchers. All those involved were deeply engaged in the work itself. Our findings are offered to fellow-practitioners, not as easy answers but as help and encouragement in a difficult and worthwhile undertaking. We believe that we have helped to change teachers' habits and improved the learning experiences and success of students. We are proud of what we have achieved and want to share it.

All three of the named authors worked together to implement the Feedback for Learning project in Winnipeg Inner City District. Authorship of the teachers' books fell to Thompson Owens, who continues to work with the teachers even after his official retirement. Authorship of this book fell to me, Ruth Sutton. Superintendent Pauline Clarke wrote the Epilogue to this book, and her influence on the books and the work they represent is immeasurable.

STAGE ONE
Starting Off

Foreword

Winnipeg Inner City School District had been pursuing a focus on assessment since 1995, and had already identified some agreed-upon assessment principles. The superintendent, Pauline Clarke, wanted this focus to continue, and was determined that the changes in teachers' assessment practices would be sustained beyond the life of the project itself. The district's Assessment Group invited an external consultant to help, who was interested in the change process as well as the assessment focus. The external consultant was, and still is, Ruth Sutton.

One necessary feature for sustainability would be the involvement of teachers as adult learners. To this end, some choices were built into the project design, making it more complicated logistically, but more likely to last. Inner City schools were invited to be involved. We explained the 'bottom line' to school leaders so they knew what they were facing: this would be a slow change process; the external consultant would visit three times each year for three years; and each school would have two days' worth of her time in each visit. Thompson Owens, the Inner City support teacher responsible for classroom assessment development, would visit schools and support teachers in-between Ruth Sutton's visits. This would provide six opportunities for the teachers to reflect on their work and decide their next steps. Six schools chose to be involved in the first year. We called these the 'first-wave' schools. We asked for a minimum of four volunteer teachers in each school, but usually there were more, between six and eight.

In each school, we began with a whole-school in-service, to enable the teachers to make good choices about involvement, and to avoid the development of an elite group and an 'out-crowd'. During the course of the year we encountered some difficulties:

- We had to clarify that this was about classroom assessment and school change, not the 'Ruth Sutton project,' based on the work of one person with the schools as relatively passive recipients of external expertise.

- We realized that teachers needed time away from the classroom to think about their strategies and to find the right starting points.

- We should have focused earlier and more sharply on gathering evidence of these strategies and their impact on learning, in order to identify the teachers' next steps.

We addressed the challenges and refined our work and focus. The following provides the results of our consultations and experience.

The newly appointed principal wanted her teachers to be learners, but found them reluctant to try new things, probably because the previous school leadership had created a culture of caution and competitive self-consciousness. She took a drastic step and announced she was about to start learning to play the trombone, and intended to share her progress with the whole school in assembly once a month.

On the first occasion, the staff watched horror-struck as the tuneless fumblings unfolded, and the children giggled and covered their ears. By the second month, after perseverance and practise, the performance had noticeably improved. By the third month, the children were so impressed that there was a ripple of applause. At the final performance of the year, the school rose in recognition of the progress made and the courage it had taken to demonstrate the learning process so publicly.

Of course, this wasn't really about playing the trombone: the principal was modelling courage, risk taking, self-belief, and perseverance, and challenging the teachers to join the learning club. For the children, especially those who were struggling, the message was very strong: learning is hard and we're all in it together.

Task, Intent, and Criteria

Stage One introduces some of the concepts of assessment strategies and explains how a school leader can begin to develop the link between classroom assessment and improved student learning. Seven sections follow:

1. how to understand the principles of assessment for learning, their origins, and their implications for classroom assessment strategies

2. how to begin the assessment process by checking the assessment strategies already in use in your school, and checking your prior experience of whole-school change

3. how to provide teachers with the information and support they need to make a start

4. how to find people and resources to help, within the school and beyond

5. how to handle the different purposes of assessment

6. how to 'lead' the process at this stage, not just 'manage' it

7. how to plan to change teaching habits

The intent of all these sections is to encourage you to think and plan your approach to implementing these strategies. When you have finished reading, you should be clear about assessment for learning, and how to introduce it in your school.

The Principles of Assessment for Learning

The first and most important understanding is that assessment *for* learning (AFL) is different from assessment *of* learning (AOL). We use the same word, *assessment*, to describe two quite different processes (see figure 1.1). Most adults, including, of course, the parents of children now in school, experienced only assessment of learning when they were in school and college themselves. No wonder there's some confusion about it.

Assessment OF Learning	Assessment FOR Learning
Looks backwards: checks learning to date	Looks forwards: used to decide next steps in learning and teaching
Audience is beyond the school	Audience is students and teachers in the classroom
Timing: periodic	Timing: continual
Uses mostly scores, grades, and percentages	Uses specific words to provide feedback
Relates to criteria and standards	Relates to student's progress
No need to involve the student	Essential to involve the student

Figure 1.1 Different purposes of assessment.

These two purposes both have a place and a role in our schools. They are not better or worse than each other: they are different. For many years, teachers, schools, and school systems have paid most attention to assessment of learning, in the belief that this will most help to improve the performance of both teachers and their students. Over the past 20 years or so, this assumption has been challenged by research about how to more effectively link assessment in our schools to the improvements in learning we all seek.

In 1988, an academic analysis was published, based on all the international research over the previous decade into the link between assessment and learning (Crooks, 1988). Some very interesting conclusions emerged, but the political climate at the time was more interested in testing and the publication of results as the means of generating improvements. Ten years later, in 1998, the same research analysis was repeated, including all the research in the intervening decade. Very similar conclusions were drawn, and this time they were communicated more clearly and reached a wider audience.

The clearest summary of the "principles" linking assessment to improved learning is identified below in figure 1.2.

The Big 5 Principles

1. The provision of effective feedback to students

2. The active involvement of students in their own learning

3. The adjustment of teaching to take into account the results of assessment

4. The recognition of the profound influence assessment has on the motivation and self-esteem of students, both of which are critical influences on learning

5. The acknowledgement of the need for students to be able to assess themselves and understand how to improve

Figure 1.2 The Big 5 Principles. *Assessment Reform Group, 1999.*

The words are taken from the pamphlet *Assessment for Learning*, published by the United Kingdom Assessment Reform Group in 1999. Some of them require a little further explanation. What is meant by "effective feedback," for example? We know that all learners benefit from feedback that is *timely, related to clear criteria, specific, constructive*, and *followed through*. There's nothing mysterious or esoteric about this. The questions are: how do students receive such feedback, and what are the implications for teachers and teaching to enable them to do so?

Implications for classroom assessment strategies

If you analyze the principles of assessment for learning, the implications for teaching and learning begin to emerge. Here are a few of them. As you read, think about the habits of planning and teaching in your school. What may need to change?

- Teachers should be clear about their expectations and the criteria by which the students' work will be judged, and share these with their students.

- Teachers should plan to provide time and coaching for their students to critique and correct their own and each other's work as part of their learning.

- Teachers should consider how to use assessment and feedback to motivate their students.

- Teachers should incorporate sufficient space and flexibility into their plans to adjust to the results of assessment: the purpose of the plan changes from 'coverage' to 'learning'.

- Teachers should involve their students more in how their learning is organized, structured, checked, and reported.

- Teachers should motivate students to acquire both the skills and the will to take more responsibility for their own learning.

- Teachers should teach the habits of self-correction early in the students' learning lives and use them at every grade level.

- Teachers should encourage students to be less dependent on their teachers to manage their learning.

- Teachers should expect students to reflect regularly on their own learning and progress.

Evidence that AFL strategies are in place

Sometimes it is easier to envisage the implications of successful implementation of assessment strategies through the concrete changes, such as the following, visible and audible as you walk around the school.

- At the beginning of the teaching module, teachers explain and explore their learning expectations with the students, and these will probably be posted somewhere in the room for regular reference as the work progresses. The criteria for successful achievement of the learning objectives will be part of the clarification, developed in a timely way and not necessarily right at the start of the work. These, too, will probably be posted or available in other ways so that the visual learners can remember them.

- The teacher will be asking more questions than before, to involve the students in thinking about their work and taking greater responsibility. For example, the student asks, "Is this finished?" and the teacher asks back, "What do you think? Have you looked at the criteria we talked about? Is there anything you still need to do, or do better?"

- Teachers and students talk together about what the students should do if they get 'stuck'. Rather than just wait for the teacher's help, they will use strategies to help themselves, such as reading over the problem again, asking someone else, or looking around the room or in their books to find ideas about what to do. The list of such agreed "strategies for getting unstuck" would be on the wall, with "Ask the teacher" right at the bottom of the list, when everything else has been tried.

- The teacher's questions are well planned and searching, pushing students towards higher order thinking. You might expect to see/hear Bloom's taxonomy being occasionally referred to in teacher conversation, or even posted somewhere: it is half a century old, but many updated versions exist and it is still a useful way to check the level of challenge in our classrooms.

- Students will have regular opportunities to reflect on and critique their own and each other's work. This feedback is not general; it is about specific things, both positive and critical. It is not a special event, but just the way the classroom works. It may be five minutes at the end of the day, or 15 minutes at the end of a unit. It could be done through a whole-class discussion, or a question-and-answer session, or a reflection sheet to be completed by the students after some discussion in a small group.

- Occasionally, the students are invited to present their work to someone else. This could be to others in the class, from another class, their parents, or other visitors to the school. This shows that the students are prepared to 'own' their work and take some pride in it.

Look and listen to any student-involved or student-led conferences going on in the school: how was the evidence they are presenting gathered and by whom? How clear and confident are the students presenting their own work? How precise are they in determining the specific next steps they need to take?

Current Assessment Practice

Researchers often comment that schools seem to know more about good assessment practice than they actually adopt in their classrooms. This could be because many of the assessment for learning strategies seem like common sense, and we assume, therefore, that they are going on all the time. The fact is, however, that some of our assessment habits were developed before we knew much about effective assessment. Our habits have not yet caught up with our knowledge.

It is important to consider how assessment actually does work, and how it can be more effectively implemented. The following provides a model for a whole-staff activity to explore the assessment starting points.

- Arrange the teaching staff – and the support staff, too, if they want to be involved – into discussion groups of four or five people. If the school is large enough, and people feel most comfortable at their own grade level, then these might be grade-level groups. In smaller schools, or if there is a more confident culture, the groups might represent different grade levels. In very small schools, the whole staff might work as one group, but with more than eight or so people, the quality of conversation might suffer.

- Focus on one or two aspects of assessment and ask people to share the specifics of what they do. For example, ask: "How do we make sure that the students understand what good work looks like, preferably before they start the task? How do we provide feedback to the students that encourages and enables them to correct their own work?"

- Give people time, and some support from a group leader if they need one, to share what they do, and to show examples of the techniques or graphic organizers they use.

- Ask for examples from each group, making a list and eliciting more information as required. The responses for clarification should be explicit. Ask: "What exactly do you say to your students when you want them to assess each other's work? Exactly when do you give the students that graphic organizer? Is it the same one for all the students?" By asking people to be explicit, you can avoid assumptions and euphemisms that can obscure real understanding when teachers talk together about their work. You can also bypass the false modesty and self-consciousness that seem to overtake some people when sharing their practice with others. Some wonderful teachers do not bother to explain what they do because they assume everyone does it, or because they do not want to be seen as boasting.

- When you have some specific information about what really happens, then refer to some of the principles of assessment for learning, in a form that suits you, and ask people to compare their current practice to what the theory suggests. "Which of those Big 5 Principles are we doing well, and which are still pretty rare?" Or look at the Winnipeg scaffolding or the rubrics in the teachers' books in this series. Use them like a template: what does the comparison tell you?

Starting with the practical experience and then analyzing it is a classic first step in experiential adult learning. As you will see in the diagram below (figure 1.3), the analysis can lead you to rethink the framework of ideas that will drive your decisions about next steps.

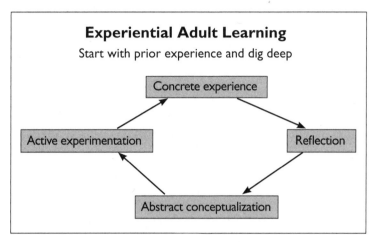

Figure 1.3 The Kolb model of experiential learning (1984).

Reflect on past experience

It is important to reflect on your past experience with assessment. This is all part of knowing your starting points and clearing the decks, ready for action. Investing time in *thinking* at this stage could save you time for *doing* later.

All of us, at one time or another, in this school or a previous one, have experienced the attempt to improve classroom practice. We might have been in the driving seat before, checking the route and at the controls, or in the passenger seat, with a good view but not contributing very much. We might have been huddled in the back seat, being thrown from side to side as the change process hurtles along, and feeling pretty queasy. Or, bored by the tediously slow pace, we have been asking the adult version of the age-old question, "Are we there yet?"

Schools are full of people who have had this experience, and now we need to discover what experience has taught us. Then we might avoid the unproductive ways of working and find more quickly the methods that will be most helpful.

In groups again, ask your teachers to consider the following questions, individually at first, and then sharing their recollections with the rest of the group: "Think for a few minutes about your previous experience of attempts to improve classroom practice. What was the goal of the change – what were you trying to do, or being asked to do? Did it succeed, and was it sustained after the first few weeks or months? If so, what happened or what was done to make it successful and sustainable? Be as explicit and specific as you can. If the change was unsuccessful, why did it fail?"

From the group's combined experience, some practical guidelines can be developed for implementing successful change. Try to avoid jargon and euphemisms, and persuade the group to express what they want to say as simply and clearly as possible.

When each group has decided on its suggestions for implementing successful change, ask each group in turn for one or two suggestions at a time, until all the guidelines have been elicited. If something is mentioned several times, it's clearly significant. When the list is complete, write down the suggestions and keep them, or post them, so that you have some "process benchmarks" to check against as you work on implementing changes in your classroom assessment practice.

This exercise will provide really useful information for you, as the leader of this change process. It will also honour the experience of your colleagues and help them to feel included in the design of implemented assessment strategies.

Find connections with other classroom strategies

Here again, we are trying to be smart about change, by finding any useful connections between the aspects of teaching we are looking at this time and those we may have tackled before.

The example to illustrate this comes straight out of our experience in Winnipeg, Manitoba. For the past few years, before the Feedback for Learning project got underway in the district, there had been an ongoing in-service focus on Understanding by Design (UBD). This is a method of curriculum planning developed by Grant Wiggins and Jay McTighe (2005) in the United States. This strategy encourages teachers to think about the 'Big Questions' that underpin a particular unit and then use 'Backwards Design' to create the teaching activities that will lead students toward the answers.

Creating Independent Student Learners

As soon as we began to work with teachers on Feedback for Learning, we asked them what they wanted their students to learn, and how they would develop the criteria that would guide the students towards success. The questions we asked the teachers were very similar to the questions underpinning Understanding by Design. It was the teachers who first pointed out the connection. They had worked on UBD before. It was clear that they understood our questions about assessment more quickly than other teachers who had not practised working this way.

> It would have been really useful if we had realized the connection earlier between the process of UBD, with which some teachers were familiar, and our Feedback for Learning process. That is why we suggest that you think about the aspects of teaching you have tackled before and that people have been thinking about, even if their practice of the techniques may have faded a bit over time. If you can make those connections, you receive a double bonus: first, some of the best of previous practice is revitalized; and, second, the adoption of the current ideas is faster and more efficient.

Adopting new classroom practice is an example of adult learning: we should treat it just as we would manage learning for our younger learners. Start where the learners are and build on what they already know and can do. That way, learning is faster, stronger, and more likely to be sustained – just as important for teachers as it is for their students.

Teachers are learners, not just employees. Successful adult learning is not just about compliance. For as long we can, with as many of our colleagues as is possible, our goal is to achieve change through intrinsic rather than extrinsic motivation. The first step is to identify prior learning and plan from there.

Helping Teachers through the Early Stages

So far you have thought carefully about the classroom assessment changes you want to implement across the school. You have reviewed the school's prior experience of change, to ensure that you learn from mistakes and find a way of working that has a chance of success. You have also made connections with other aspects of teaching with which your school has been working.

Now we consider how you provide the information, support, and resources that teachers will need to make a start on introducing AFL in their classrooms. It is sensible to start with a small number of classrooms and encourage change to spread like a virus, exponentially, until all, or almost all, the teachers are involved. In the next section, we will discuss how you decide which teachers will be your 'pioneers' and which will be more comfortable as 'settlers'.

Even though you will focus on a small number of classrooms in the early stages of change, there are good reasons for offering information about the proposed changes in assessment practice – both the content and the process – to all your teaching and support staff, and to parents, too. You are signalling that this work is of great importance: it will drive the school for a number of years and will eventually become an integral part of the way the school does business. The way the ideas are introduced really does matter.

The first step is one of the hardest. If the introduction of the ideas goes well, you can move on with confidence. If it does not, the experience is almost worse than nothing happening at all, as a bad first experience could make teachers reluctant to try again. The following is a brief checklist about the decisions you must make.

- **Who should be given access to the first stage of sharing ideas and direction?** We suggest that should be all the adults – teachers, support staff, and parents – but not necessarily all at once. Involving teachers and support staff first, together, and then parents later would be our suggestion, but you know your school and what has worked before for you. We believe it is important that school staff are really clear themselves about the purpose, strategies, and implications of assessment before they attempt to explain their issues to parents and the community.

- **Do you have an opportunity to present the same message to all the adults who work with students in your classrooms?** A shared and unmixed message reduces the possibility of different interpretations of the same ideas. It also signals that this will ultimately be a whole-school change. If the only access you have to everyone is in an after-school staff meeting, wait until a daytime opportunity can be found, probably an in-service day. We are all aware that the 'twilight slot' after school is not the best time for presenting new and challenging ideas. In most schools by mid-afternoon, the intellectual lights are switched off and the building as a learning environment is half-empty, even if everyone is still there.

- **Who can help with the first introduction of the ideas?** Here again, you must signal the importance of what is being presented without people's feeling this is coming at them from outside. If you use an outside consultant, do so sparingly, and always partner them with an insider, someone known to the school and trusted by teachers. Sometimes schools want to begin by sending staff to a consultant's lectures, but beware. We know that the actual impact of those events is minimal: change happens only if there is immediate and well-planned follow-up back at school. If the shared experience has been positive, you have a window of opportunity to cash in on the 'feel good factor'. If it has not been a good experience, then you have a bigger hill to climb to convince people that the ideas are worthy of their extended attention.

- **How will you provide teachers with the opportunity to discuss the implications for teaching and learning that arise from these principles, and to make the connections between abstract theory and the realities of their teaching lives?** Some teachers will realize they already use some of these principles. Much of effective teaching is intuitive: good teachers do things that feel 'right'. We need to recognize this, and applaud it, but you cannot build a whole-school approach to teaching on intuition alone. The research evidence may sound dry and detached from reality, but it does represent a significant body of evidence, gathered from all over the world over more than 20 years. Intuition supported by such evidence is a powerful basis for change.

- **How will this first encounter with the principles and their implications accommodate the different learning styles of your teachers?** Many school leaders think it is helpful to provide lots of reading material, but we have discovered in working with teachers how few of them actually learn through reading. For the Winnipeg project, we purchased books for the first group of teachers involved, and special three-ring binders to hold the other materials we supplied. When we checked later about who had actually used them, very few teachers had done so.

Make written resources available for the school staff library, or keep them until someone asks a question that indicates curiosity and readiness to investigate further, when that spark can be fanned by the prompt provision of the right resource. The type of written resource matters, too: very few teachers not engaged in full-time professional study have the time and inclination to plough through heavy literature. We found a wealth of resources that proved very useful, listed in Further Reading at the end of this book, and the collection is expanding all the time.

Access to expert help

However effective your school's first exposure to the principles of assessment for learning may have been, what matters more is the steady growth of understanding linked to the realities of the classroom over the months and even years that follow. Given the parameters of money and time available, school leaders must decide how best to give teachers access to the support they will need. Later on in this section, we will look at how the on-site leaders can best support the work. If you do have outside expertise available to you, from the school district, for example, decide how to use this as a resource in your school.

It is tempting (and less expensive) to avoid the need for substitute teachers by having the consultant visit the teacher in the classroom and do the coaching and conversation in situ. This allows for observation and modelling, and, at later stages in the learning process, this may well be useful. But at this early stage, the classroom is simply too busy to allow the teacher to focus. Try to give teachers opportunity for conversation away from the classroom for a while. Allow time for deep reflection that will, in turn, support the teachers' understanding of why and how to change their practice.

In the Feedback for Learning project, two support people were available to help teachers and schools during the first three years of the work. Ruth Sutton was a consultant already known to the Inner City school leaders, but not familiar to the teachers. The other person was a district support teacher, Thompson Owens, who had worked in the district for 30 years, first as a teacher and, more recently, supporting teachers in Language Arts and curriculum planning. He has had training in the Understanding by Design process and had led the district's previous success in developing its shared Assessment Principles, providing the base on which Feedback for Learning as a district-wide project was built. He was well known and respected by all the teachers with whom we worked.

Thompson and Ruth tried to have a useful conversation with every teacher involved in the work, about once every six weeks. Schools sometimes hired a substitute teacher for the whole day. The substitute teacher moved from room to room, allowing each teacher in turn to be released for a teaching period to have very high-quality talking and planning time with either one or both of the external supporters. In some schools, a combination of substitute teachers and internal reshuffling of teachers and students allowed a group of teachers to be released together for an hour, or even longer.

Every conversation with teachers, individually or in small groups, began with questions about the assessment strategies they had been trying in their classes. We asked questions such as: "What's working? What exactly do you do? Why do you think it's working? What have you been struggling with? How can we help you? What will you try next? When should one of us talk to you again?" Of course, consultants can suggest ideas, but these will only be effective if the teacher decides to try them. As much as possible, when interviewing teachers about their work, it helps to have them decide what to do next. Knowing that they would be asked the same questions the next time we met added enough motivation for teachers to keep their progress going. Anyone working with teachers, especially in the challenging conditions of the inner city, must recognize just how hard the job is, and the courage and energy it takes to change daily habits of teaching.

This is not an inexpensive model of teacher development. If consultants must be paid, you may worry about their spending time with just a few teachers. If you take the teacher out of the classroom for these conversations, you may have to pay for cover teachers, or juggle classes to give the teacher some time away from their room. In Winnipeg, very little money was available from the district to help schools with these costs, and they were expected to find most of the funding from within their existing in-service budget. However, not being allocated extra temporary funding from the school district or any other source meant that schools knew from the start that they would be allocating their own money, time, and priorities to a different purpose. Because there was no additional money, there was no stage at which the extra funding disappeared. It is at this point that many initiatives fail, and the attention moves on to the next initiative with extra funding. We were looking for permanent change in classroom practice, and not having additional money was one way for schools to achieve it.

One further observation about our conversations with the project teachers: these opportunities meant a great deal to the teachers involved, as many of them told us. They felt valued, listened to, supported, and encouraged to reflect deeply on how they teach and to take risks in trying new techniques. That was the only purpose of our time together. There was no other agenda, no assumptions, no judgment, and ample opportunity to communicate in the ways that best suited the teachers. The conversations were private and removed from the distractions of the classroom. Administrators trusted that we were not wasting the time that was found at such expense to the school, and teachers felt they were learning in a highly effective way.

At the end of every meeting, goals were established, which were followed through and discussed when we met again. For example, a teacher might decide to try building a rubric with students rather than designing it herself. Another teacher might decide to introduce the task and intent at the beginning of a unit and then, at the end of each teaching period, review progress of the task and intent. Six weeks later, the teachers would report how their goals had been achieved and identify their next steps. The same progress towards sustainable change could not have been made without these focused conversations, costly though they were.

Keep the whole school informed

In all Winnipeg schools we worked with, except the very smallest where all the teachers were involved in classroom change, we suggested that all teaching and support staff be kept informed about the progress their colleagues were making.

This has several positive aspects: first, it respects the teachers' basic need to be kept informed. Second, it enables those teachers who haven't originally volunteered to join the 'active' group. This unofficial route to full participation can happen quite regularly as more cautious teachers discover through conversation with their colleagues that the strategies they were trying were manageable and did actually work, for the teachers as well as the students. The 'first-wave' active teachers sometimes wanted specific others – particular friends or prospective work partners – to join them.

For example, the teacher who has been trying to involve students in developing a rubric will probably talk to other teachers about this and what happened. Other teachers will know the students involved, and may be curious about how they responded. If it worked well, the other teachers might be encouraged to try something similar. If it didn't, the original teacher might ask for advice from others who have tried something similar. Sometimes the students enjoy an activity and tell other teachers about it, or ask the teacher to do something similar with them. This kind of informal communication about the work is very useful, although generally as an adjunct to other strategies.

The third positive reason for keeping communication going between the active people and the rest of the staff is that it supports the development of the involved teachers as they articulate their learning to their peers. "See one, do one, teach one" is the medical school mantra about learning new procedures; coaching someone else is an indication that your own learning has progressed.

To allow for that to happen, in Winnipeg we faced the age-old problem called in New Zealand the "tall poppy syndrome." In some community cultures, and in some school micro-cultures, it appears unacceptable for someone to share their own positive experience with others without implicitly criticizing them. Any tall poppy whose head sticks up above the crop will be quickly mown down.

We were regularly surprised at the reluctance of fine teachers to 'lead' their colleagues, even by example. We tried to use the term *lead teachers* to describe those actively involved in the first year of the Winnipeg project, but this title was rejected by all of them, and replaced by *Feedback for Learning teachers* or some other more descriptive title. Obviously, the disposition to be reflective and seek improvement in one's own work is different from the disposition to present oneself confidently to one's peers. Some of the finest teachers we worked with were very reluctant to present their learning to others. Some of them, too, were operating intuitively, which made them excellent teachers, but also inhibited their ability to articulate what they did and why they did it. For these intuitive teachers, our work and conversations enabled them to underpin their intuition, to strengthen their confidence, and to provide the language they needed to describe their decisions and actions to others.

Whatever they were called, the first-wave teachers were given opportunities to share their work, at staff meetings or grade-level meetings or as part of an in-service day. Their own peers are always the hardest audience for any teacher; some of them said it was far easier to talk to teachers from other schools, but that would not have achieved the other objective of keeping their colleagues informed. Later in the work, we did establish visits to other schools as part of the teachers' development, and arranged for them to come together occasionally from all the schools to share ideas.

That was in Winnipeg schools, in the first year of our work. Your choices will be informed by your own circumstances, here and now. By whatever means you can, keep the whole school informed about what is happening. It is important to avoid a growing distance between the cognoscenti and the 'also-rans'.

Find the Right People

All the current theories regarding change suggest that sustainable change cannot be just driven by the leader from the top down. This is especially true in schools: teaching is a relatively private activity that cannot be continually monitored. Its success depends on the ongoing behaviour of the teacher, interacting with learning and learners all the time, often behind a closed door.

In these circumstances, school leaders should recognize that a number of people are required to work toward change. It is unlikely that everyone will come on-board simultaneously, as all their starting points are different. A smaller subset of the whole staff might be the 'pioneers' opening up the way to encourage the 'settlers' to come along behind once the landscape has been mapped and the ground has been cleared a little. One of the most important choices the school leader makes is the choice of pioneers. In the jargon of change theory, this is about "distributing the leadership."

In some schools the choices are limited. In very small schools, everyone might choose – or feel obliged by peer pressure – to be involved all at once. But in larger schools, or those with a wider range of approaches, the possibilities are more varied and may include the following scenarios.

- **Issue an open invitation:** invite everyone to be involved, and wait for the enthusiasts to volunteer.

- **Use existing structures:** all those with an existing group leadership responsibility are expected to be involved, whether they wish to be or not.

- **Shoulder-tap:** identify the people who would be most likely to succeed, and whom the rest of the staff respect, and ask them to 'volunteer', with or without promises of various incentives (for example, more in-service, some extra time to do the work, because they are being evaluated this year, as a trade-off for something they want from you). The list of possible incentives is long and potentially devious, designed to press the particular buttons of whomever you want to enlist.

If you are going to choose a group, consider the criteria carefully. You need someone with some existing expertise and confidence in the area, who is also able to be patient with less gifted colleagues. You need someone who is clearly not a 'bandwagon' person, and whose views are respected by the staff. You need someone who sees potential pitfalls as well as the positives. You need someone who is able to connect with you as the school leader and to see the big picture. All your leaders need the capacity to work hard, not just relying on the energy of others. The group must be large enough to sustain a pool of energy and ideas, and to survive someone's being absent or leaving the group.

One note of caution. When a group of teachers is brought together, by whatever means, to do some work on behalf of the school, the group may be less effective than the sum of its parts, because of the climate and internal dynamic of the group. It helps to consider the dynamic when you decide who you want to be involved, and to pay attention to the forming and early work of the group, to ensure that they find a productive way of working together. We know that students need to have guidelines for effective group work. Adult learners can benefit from such guidelines, too, and it is worth suggesting that they agree on these before they start work.

And a final note of caution. Some excellent teachers work more effectively with students than they do with other adults. A very vociferous person might need to be placed in a group with someone else who can stand up to them and prevent them from dominating the group.

Different Purposes of Assessment

Right at the beginning of this book, we considered the various purposes of assessment. These purposes require different strategies, and appeal to different audiences. At a theoretical level, it is interesting to see how these pieces of the assessment jigsaw fit together. The current climate of schooling creates serious tensions regarding the purpose and practice of assessment, despite the mounting evidence that our traditional approaches have not been as effective as was hoped in raising standards of teaching and learning in our schools.

Let's take a look at how assessment is perceived. These perceptions are often confused and controversial; all the more reason to take them seriously. Problems arise from the use of the word *assessment* itself. Although it originally meant "to sit alongside," from the Latin *assidere*, it has been loaded with other definitions and connotations for the past few hundred years. Now it is inextricably linked in our minds with judgment, and, more particularly, negative judgment. It has also been loaded with expectations of statistical measurement, comparisons, and, most recently, with accountability. In practical terms, and in the experience of most people educated in the English-speaking world over the past 50 years, it means *testing*. No wonder, for many people, including many teachers and parents, it conjures discomfort, anxiety, and an impression that we only value what we can count.

No wonder, either, that we made an early decision in Winnipeg to avoid the word *assessment* in the naming of our work. To remove any confusion over our goals and strategies, we adopted the title *Feedback for Learning*. The title does not necessarily capture the wealth of classroom practice involved in the work, but neither would any other.

Assessment *for* learning is entirely different from assessment *of* learning, but unfortunately, despite the richness of our language, we have failed to develop a different word to allocate to those practices in which we use our judgment and feedback to improve learning rather than just measure it. Refer to figure 1.1 for a reminder of the distinction between assessment *for* learning and assessment *of* learning that we provided earlier.

Both these purposes are of legitimate importance to schools. Schools reflect the values of the communities they serve, are funded by them, and agree to meet their needs. One of these needs is to guide young people towards further education and employment, and another is to enable providers of those services to understand what the young people know and can do. Until the very end of schooling, when this need is most acute, the driving principle of schooling must be to *develop* learning, not just calibrate it. Hence, the growing interest in those strategies – which we still call *assessment* – that help learners to understand and take responsibility for their own progress.

We cannot expect that in the complexity of modern schooling, those functions can be sealed off from each other and never interact. Our accountability to parents drives us to periodically gather information about learning, as a series of snapshots, and to communicate this as meaningfully as we can. Traditionally, parents have been offered measurements of their children's learning and comparisons with other children, and this is still what many parents expect.

The pressure to use measurement rather than developmental assessment techniques filters down into the earlier years of schooling. In North America, the parental expectation of information seems ever more insistent, perhaps as we have all been offered more and more information, more frequently available, in other areas of our lives. Reporting to parents, therefore, sits uneasily between assessment of learning and assessment for learning, and creates a confusion of purpose in many schools. Another increasing interest is in gathering and tracking information about student learning at the system level, usually to identify and rectify under-performance by schools and teachers. This is not the place to debate the various merits or otherwise of the purpose and impact of large-scale assessment, but the existence of these practices forms the inevitable backdrop to the development of more learning-focused assessment, such as Winnipeg's Feedback for Learning project.

Many of you reading about the importance of assessment for learning will already be involved – whether you like it or not – in province-wide testing. In Manitoba, school divisions were, at the time of our project, able to opt out of the provincial requirements and to create their own assessment procedures. Winnipeg School Division took this option, and the Comprehensive Assessment Program (CAP) was started in all schools in 2000.

In those early years in Winnipeg's Inner City District schools, school leaders had to accommodate both the Feedback for Learning and the CAP in their strategic thinking and try to weave them together. The purpose of the CAP was to derive reliable information about students' literacy, numeracy, learning, and social skills. The CAP was, therefore, about assessment of learning, even though its outcomes should be used to improve teaching. Feedback for Learning, on the other hand, aims to improve the quality and independence of the learning, not to measure. Leaders of Feedback for Learning had to manage CAP and FFL simultaneously, and found it quite a challenge at the beginning. If you are faced with managing these two purposes simultaneously, here is some advice about how to do so.

The first essential is to be very clear in your own mind, and to be prepared to share with your community, that the overriding purpose of schooling is to develop student learning. Nothing must be allowed to interfere with that goal. With that in mind, we can focus on the characteristics of all our professional activity that lead towards the goal. "Keep your eyes on the prize," runs the slogan, and the prize is all our students as learners, in school and for the rest of their lives.

In order to achieve maximum learning, we must engage the motivation and aspirations of our students as well as their cognitive abilities. We recognize that learning habits matter, and know that these may be as hard to change once they have developed as our own habits are, so we start the habits of involvement and responsibility for learning as early as we can. Assessment for learning is not about 'events' in the same way assessment of learning is, so the two can be handled quite differently. An event is planned into the school's calendar, but the process of assessment and feedback for learning is part of the fabric of the classroom, minute by minute.

When you are developing your school's action plan or strategic development plan, keep the two strands of the assessment processes distinct in your plan, with specific success indicators linked to each and an evaluation strategy designed to discover those indicators and reflect on them. In Stage Three we will consider how to build assessment development into your school's action plan.

It is important to remember that it is possible to use a strategy required by assessment of learning, a test or a report, to support learning as well as measure it. Having the students write a contribution to their own report, based on review and reflection about achievement in class, and including their specific learning goals for the following weeks, could make the report useful to the student as well as to the parent. Doing a practice test and then reviewing how the students tackled it, having them work together to correct their mistakes, and reflecting on how they can approach tasks more successfully – all that helps learning, too. Once we understand the principles of assessment for learning, and above all the need to involve the students themselves, we can find many ways to accommodate those principles even in climates dominated by tests and accountability. What you have to watch out for is: "Yes, we'd love to involve the students, but we don't have time as we're too busy covering everything for the test." That's a classic example of misguided thinking: involving the students and getting better test results are not mutually exclusive, but integrally linked. Involving the students is a key way to enhance the performance of many students, and especially those who are not going to be very successful in normative terms.

How to Lead, Rather than Manage

To this point, the "expected behaviours" for school leaders have involved thinking hard about the starting point of the school, the support and resources required and the people to be involved. The following are additional suggestions about what to do at this stage.

- There may be people helping your teachers to adopt new assessment strategies. If you do not have the time or opportunity to find out exactly what these people are doing, do try to see the teachers from time to time to ask about their activities. A dedicated meeting is the most desirable, but, otherwise, a casual passing enquiry can often be just as effective, so long as your curiosity is genuine and you listen with care and ask good follow-up questions. It is the details that are interesting. The question to ask is not "Did you explain to the students the expectations in that task?" but "*How* did you explain to the students the expectations in that task?" Ask the teacher how best to share the information they have about their practice and process.

- Integrate the principles and language of assessment of learning into your own practice. Here is one example: at the beginning of each staff meeting, a principal we worked with began by explaining the learning objectives of the meeting and the criteria for successful achievement of those objectives, and then returned to those for review in the last few minutes – just as we would want a teacher to do in the classroom. Here is another example: having learned about providing good feedback in the classroom, the principal amended his feedback to teachers after classroom observation and evaluations, to improve its quality and impact.

- Begin to incorporate the expectations regarding teaching and assessing for learning into the criteria for classroom observations and evaluation. All school leaders have a responsibility to evaluate teachers from time to time. This is an assessment process, but is it assessment of teaching or assessment for teaching? If we want to improve the quality of teaching, not just to measure it, then school leaders should consider the Big 5 Principles (see figure 1.2) and apply them to the teacher evaluation process.

In Winnipeg, the criteria for teacher evaluation were determined at the division level, and the central involvement of the Inner City District Superintendent enabled these expectations to be built into the revised teacher evaluation process. A rubric of professional standards contains several references to the kinds of assessment practices teachers are expected to include in their classrooms.

- Make it clear that you are a learner, too. We all begin by focusing on the students as learners. To do this, we must develop our teachers as learners, willing and able to take a risk to try new things, to stumble sometimes and learn more from the experience, and to move on. To complete the circle of learning in the school, the principal should be a full member of the learning club, as prepared as anyone else to take a risk and try new things, knowing that new ideas sometimes will not be completely successful the first time.

- Be patient. If changing teachers' classroom practice were easy, you would not be reading this. You can post the criteria for effective group work, but unless they are developed with the students and then used to help them critique their own achievement in group work, they are just cosmetic. Perhaps because we have chased too many initiatives and expect them to last a year or so before they are superseded by the next one, we may be tempted to expect too much progress too quickly and be disappointed at the relatively slow pace. Many principals struggle with teachers who take a while to decide what to do and how to do it. Of course, sometimes the slow pace of change is an indication of reluctance to make any change at all, but most often this is not the case, and you need only to be patient and encouraging. Our experience with changing classroom practice is that it is about changing habits: planning, questioning, marking and grading, demanding higher order thinking of both yourself and the students. Those habits were acquired slowly through practice and experience, and they are likely to change the same way.

Helping your teachers to change their habits will involve you in providing them with effective feedback, just as you want them to provide feedback for their students. This is your chance to model assessment for learning principles yourself. Look for the small indications that a teacher's practice is changing. Recognize and encourage them, and give them time. If criteria start to appear on the wall of the classroom, ask how they are being developed and used. If a teacher starts to have an end-of-day or end-of-lesson review with her students, ask her about the questions she is using to prompt reflection and what she notices about the outcomes. If you talk to students about their work, ask if they know what to do next to improve their learning and notice how specific they are in reply. All these are the indicators you need in order to know that progress is being made, however slowly.

Of course, even committed teachers stall and struggle at times. Meeting report deadlines, for example, can drive the new habit to the back of the mind. Many teachers prefer to start new habits with their students at the beginning of a new school session rather than in the middle. It is important to keep asking the questions about intentions and ideas.

Strategic Planning to Change Habits

The Feedback for Learning team discussed and researched the literature on the role of the limbic brain in changing adult habits. The thesis is simple: teaching – and leadership – are habits, learned through example and experiences over time. After a while, those habits can become hard-wired and hard to change. Our brains are divided into three parts. The neo-cortex deals with new learning, absorbing information, classifying and storing it, and recalling when the need arises. The neo-cortex is what we need when we are writing an assignment and, as teachers, we have become adept neo-cortex users. The reptilian brain is, thankfully, less used in the school environment, where the basic needs of survival and reproduction are less evident (although some schools do seem to test our survival instincts more than others). Between the two is the limbic brain, handling emotions, experiences, and habits. Here's the important thing: habits learned through the limbic brain can only be changed through the limbic brain. We can learn what to do using the neo-cortex, but if we want it to become a habit, we have to do it using the limbic.

Here is an example of how teachers' habits affect their approach to assessment. In one of the research studies in England, junior high teachers were asked to try increasing their "wait time," the time between asking questions and expecting an answer from the students. Instead of waiting less than a second, which was their normal habit, the teachers were asked to increase the wait time by five seconds.

The first time the teachers tried to change this habit, they reported physiological signs of discomfort: increased heart rate, sweating, and slight nausea. Intellectually, using the neo-cortex, the teachers understood that increasing the wait time was a good idea, as it gave students time to think and consider their response. The limbic brain's adherence to the normal habit produced the conflict and the discomfort. This is why researchers report a gap between what teachers know they should be doing and what they actually do.

How to Manage Stage One: A Summary of Advice

- Do your homework: read and understand as much of the assessment for learning ideas as you can.

- Review the starting point of assessment practice in your school and plan ahead.

- Make best use of external support and internal talent.

- Be prepared to invest resources in providing teachers with the opportunities they need to change their practice.

- Encourage sensible risk taking and model it yourself.

- Do not be blown off course by anxiety about testing and accountability.

- Get involved yourself: you are a learner, too.

- Be patient, and don't give up.

FAQs at Stage One

1. As the principal, I have to manage all aspects of the school. Isn't it more efficient to leave leadership of assessment practice to others, without getting involved in it myself?

   Assessment for learning is fundamental to the way a school conducts its core business. As such, it is important for the school leader to understand, support, and model the principles, in order to demonstrate its importance to the teachers who take their cues from what the principal does and says.

2. Only one or two teachers volunteered in my school to be involved in the first stage of introducing assessment for learning. What should I do?

You may need to slow down a little. It is a good idea to give teachers some choices regarding their involvement with assessment for learning. It is also sensible for teachers to avoid volunteering for something until they are really clear about the project to which they are committing themselves. There are potential benefits for both teachers and students. Offer the most detailed explanation you can about why and how assessment for learning could influence student learning and motivation, and make the teacher's job easier and more productive. Be clear about the support available, the time frame, and the expectations. Then, allow some time for thought. Have a private conversation with some teachers, not to coerce them but to help them explore the implications of involvement. Give people time to consider: don't expect an instant decision.

Sometimes the most capable teachers do not volunteer, which may surprise you. Consider the possible reasons for their reluctance. They may know they are good at what they do, and do not want to risk trying something new to a less than perfect standard. They may feel they are already using assessment for learning techniques intuitively and do not need to go further. They may have good reasons for not taking on extra involvement right now. If you want them to be involved, talk it through with them and respect whatever choice they make. They will want to be involved ultimately because assessment for learning demonstrably helps learning, but maybe not at first. Any change process has 'pioneers' and 'settlers': both make their contribution, in different ways.

Teachers often trust other teachers more than they trust anyone else. If you can bring in someone who has been working with assessment for learning strategies in their own classroom, and realizes the value and the positive impact on behaviour, learning, and their own job satisfaction, that person may convince teachers to join in the project.

If you still do not have more than one or two volunteers, this may be because of previous bad experience of whole-school projects. People have long memories! Find out what went wrong last time, and promise to avoid those mistakes this time.

3. Isn't assessment for learning more relevant for younger students? In high school, we have to focus on getting good grades.

One of the goals and effects of assessment for learning is to improve the students' grades. Implementation in the classroom may mean changes in the focus and purpose of teachers' planning, with less emphasis on coverage of the material and more focus on successful learning. This creates some choices for teachers in the early stages, as they slow down a little in order to ensure better learning. When the students benefit from this process and the quality of learning improves, most teachers find that the investment has paid off. By making the students more aware of what they need to do to achieve in the higher grades, providing more specific feedback, increasing their sense of control over their own performance, and providing evidence of their progress towards success, assessment for learning strategies do improve many students' grades. Not every student will benefit, but enough will do so to make a significant difference to the school's overall performance.

4. Where can high school teachers find the specific advice they need to translate assessment for learning into their circumstances?

High school teachers want specialist advice, and there are many good resources available. The best starting point we know of is Ken O'Connor's book *How to Grade for Learning* (2002). Ken is an experienced high school teacher from Ontario, and his book is clear, relevant, and very challenging, as he questions some of the common assumptions of high school assessment practice.

STAGE TWO
Consolidation and Spread

Foreword

As we moved into Stage Two, more schools joined the Feedback for Learning project in the second year, making 10 in all. New teachers also joined us in the first-wave schools, bringing the total number to around 70. With more teachers and the same level of external support, each teacher had less assistance. We tried to maintain access to the external supporters six times a year to help the new teachers, and reduced the level of support to those in their second year.

Reflecting on our experience during the first year, we made a number of adjustments.

- We introduced the scaffolding to help teachers reflect on their work and to decide where to focus their attention (see Chapter 1 of the teachers' books in this series).

- We gave more priority to making sure school leaders understood more clearly the learning needs of teachers to have time for conversation with both the 'experts' and their colleagues.

- We helped to organize meetings of teachers across the participating schools, to share ideas in a bigger 'gene pool'.

- Based on the scaffolding, and prompted by the superintendent, we developed a rubric to clarify teachers' progress in using Feedback for Learning techniques (see appendix 4 of the teachers' books in this series).

- We developed a manageable way of collecting evidence from the teachers about their strategies, their success, the evidence, the difficulties, and the next steps.

- We began to meet with the leaders of the participating schools as a separate group, and work with them on issues regarding change, to deepen our reflection about the progress of Feedback for Learning.

Meeting these challenges and adjusting our methods resulted in better communication and better understanding of the process and its implementation.

The new principal wanted to devote one in-service session to teachers sharing ideas with each other. The vice-principal told him not to bother: they had tried it once before and teachers did not respect each other's contributions. One or two people had been critical of a young teacher's efforts and it had ended acrimoniously.

The principal thought about it for a while. Then he decided that instead of avoiding the idea of teachers' professional sharing, he would actually increase its importance. His goal was to give teachers a very positive professional experience and to signal the importance he attached to the process of sharing.

He gave each grade-level team time to choose a strategy for involving students in any aspect of their teaching or classroom management, and asked them to try out their chosen strategy over a number of weeks. An expert on school-based action research was invited into the school to advise the teachers about how to conduct their 'experiment' and how to gather evidence of the impact on learning and student achievement. Each team was then asked by the principal to prepare a short presentation for their colleagues at the next in-service session, was given guidelines about how to do it, and was encouraged to aspire to a very high standard of presentation. Teachers from other schools were invited to attend.

The high value placed on the activity, the quality of the teachers' work, the high expectations of the principal, and the presence of strangers from another school all contributed to teachers demonstrating very high professional standards to each other. They surprised each other, and themselves. Each presentation was followed by questions and the principal personally thanked each team at the end of each contribution. The teachers were encouraged to behave as well as they could, and the principal's careful planning set them up to be successful. It was a great day. A precedent for professional sharing had been established and they never looked back.

Task, Intent, and Criteria

In Stage One, you were dealing with teachers who had volunteered to change their assessment practice. In Stage Two, more teachers are joining the process. Some of these will be enthusiastic pioneers who, for some reason, did not get involved earlier. Most of the teachers joining the process at this stage are more cautious: they are settlers, not pioneers, who like to know why and how they should change their practice rather than plunging ahead just to enjoy the ride.

Our task in this stage is to advise you how to take account of the greater numbers of teachers involved and their different motivations. The work begun in Stage One will be continued and deepened. Teachers will be learning from each other, and the mechanisms for doing so, therefore, will be important.

In the four sections at this stage we will address:

- how to recognize and encourage early progress

- how to connect assessment for learning with other initiatives

- how to lead and foster adult learning in your school

- how to achieve teachers' engagement, not just compliance, in changing classroom practice

Our intent is to help you through the phase of "How does it work in the second year?" when the first flush of enthusiasm is fading and other priorities may clamour for your attention. When you have finished this section you should be:

- able to recognize that assessment for learning is happening in your school

- sufficiently confident to adopt assessment for learning in the way you lead the school: clarifying expectations, organizing helpful activities for your teachers, asking pertinent questions to move the work forward

- ready to make the necessary structural and systems changes that will embed assessment for learning into your school for the longer term

Recognize and Encourage Early Progress

In the Stage One section, we offered some details about what you might expect to see in a classroom where assessment for learning was beginning. You should continue to take an interest in what is happening in classrooms, and, at this stage, you might see and hear indications of progress. We will now explore in greater detail what you might now expect to see, what it means, and what kinds of questions you could ask that reveal the teachers' intentions and possible next steps. The following are some key activities you should expect to see.

Clarification of learning objectives. As you will remember from Stage One, the first thing the teacher must do is decide and then explain to the students what he wants them to learn and how the tasks they will undertake connect to that overall objective. In the early stages, teachers find this quite difficult. They know what they want students to *do*, but are less clear sometimes about what they want them to *learn*. Test yourself: from this list, which are learning objectives and which are tasks?

a) to label the diagram of the eye
b) to improve our football passing skills
c) to understand how transport affects pollution
d) to learn to interpret pie charts
e) to complete activities 1b, 2a, and 2b from page 16 of your textbook
f) to know the characteristics of earthquakes
g) to debate whether the use of atomic weapons in 1945 was justified
h) to know how to evaluate a product against a design specification

(The answers are at the end of Stage Two.)

If you have only a few minutes to spend in someone's classroom, check whether they are explaining tasks and learning objectives to their students, and whether they are clear about this distinction.

Rubrics. A rubric is a combination of criteria (what we look for in the students' work) and standards (the quality of the achievement of each criterion). You will find an example of rubrics in appendix 4 in the teachers' books in this series and advice for teachers about how to construct and use them. When teachers begin to assess students' work against specific expectations and provide more specific feedback, they often find rubrics very useful. They are visual and concrete, and they make assessment more straightforward and clear. You will hear teachers begin to talk about rubrics, and you will see them appearing on classroom walls, to guide both teachers and students as they work. You can ask good questions now about how the rubric was developed and how it is used to make it a learning tool as well as a teaching tool. Here are some questions to ask about any rubrics you might see, both to encourage teachers to reflect on this strategy and to increase its impact on student performance.

- Who developed this rubric? How do you make sure that the students understand it?

- If you gave the students examples of completed work in this assignment, do you think they could work out the criteria and the different standards, with your help, and put the rubric together themselves?

- You're probably using a rubric about research skills every time you set the students a research task. Do you use the same rubric for that, so that they can see how their skills are improving from one research assignment to the next?

With good questions, good timing, and good listening, you can help your teachers work out how a classroom strategy, such as the use of rubrics, connects with the Big 5 Principles of assessment for learning we presented in Stage One (see figure 1.2).

Portfolios. Here is a quick definition of a portfolio: A portfolio contains selected examples of a learner's learning. Each item is chosen for a purpose, with some indication of why it was chosen and what it represents. As part of assessment for learning, a portfolio will indicate the learner's progress over time, and provide guidance about the learner's next steps.

This definition is closely linked to learning, progress, and next steps. It is different from other portfolios that are a showcase only for best work, or others that are related to external benchmarks and underpin the teacher's judgments in relation to those benchmarks.

If assessment for learning is developing in your classrooms, teachers will be talking to students about their work and the evidence of their learning. They will encourage students to review their progress and to reflect on their next steps for improvement. Periodically, teachers and students may select items of work that illustrate key aspects of learning and progress, and keep them in a folder. These items can be shared with parents or the next teacher. If your teachers are developing portfolios with their students, here are some questions you can ask about them.

- Who chose the items in the portfolio, and what do the items represent?

- Can the students explain the significance of these items, and link them to particular learning they have achieved?

- How often do you and the students decide which items to keep, and why? Does the selection occur as part of the continuing discussions about learning in your room?

Student-led conferences (SLCs). Involving the students in presenting their learning and progress to their parents is certainly not a new idea in North America. In Winnipeg Inner City District, it is the practice in all elementary schools. In addition to the normal reporting to parents conducted by every school, the student-led conference is an event where the student, guided and supported by the teacher, takes his/her parents through the portfolio, showing how learning has developed over several months and explaining the next steps necessary for further improvement. This takes organization and preparation: teachers would do it only if they were convinced that the conference would help learning and increase parental understanding of how their child is doing.

SLCs are a natural extension of assessment for learning. They epitomize the learner's involvement in self-critique, self-correction, and awareness of their own progress. If you have not yet considered such a strategy for your school, a good place to start is with Anne Davies et al.'s very helpful book *Together Is Better* (1992). If you have already started the process in your school, and want to check how well it connects to assessment for learning, here are some questions to ask.

- Who chooses the items that students will share with their parents? Do the students know why these specific items were chosen?

- Have the students been given an opportunity to rehearse in class what they want to say about these items?

- Do parents understand the purpose of this strategy, and does it help them to support their child's next steps in learning?

Student-led conferencing in secondary/high schools

Many secondary school colleagues are skeptical about student-led conferencing in post-elementary settings. Anything that elementary schools do well is sometimes suspect in secondary schools, just for that reason. "It might work with younger children," high school teachers tell us, "but, of course, it will never work here." Why not? Why do we assume that older students will not be able to do what younger students can clearly manage? It may be more about will than skill. The goal is to make student-led conferencing in high schools manageable, "cool," and entirely relevant to this stage of schooling.

Here are some suggestions for junior and senior high schools about encouraging older students to present their learning

- Redefine the purpose. For older students, learning to present their own learning is a preparation for learning after school and moving into the workplace. It represents an acceptance of adult responsibility. That is why we do it at this stage. It is never a good idea to tell older students that we are extending a good practice from elementary school: moving into junior or senior high is a "rite of passage" into adulthood for most young people and their families.

- As part of this new rationale, talk to educators from the next level of learning after the students leave your school. In college, a student's success often depends on their willingness and ability to critique and correct their own work – to be a self-managing learner. Those who supervise the progress of students at this level will testify to the importance of these skills. Similarly, those who recruit young people into the workforce, after college or before, will also understand how important it is for young people to have these skills. These people can and should speak with authority about this to students and their families. In our experience, young people have more faith in messages from outside school than they have in what the 'insiders' tell them. Use that lever: invite people from the outside community to make a presentation to your students about the skills they will need to succeed in their next working or learning environment.

- Recognize that students cannot present their own learning with any accuracy or conviction unless they have first learned how to critique and correct it. They learn these lessons in the classroom, with their teachers. If assessment for learning is not occurring in the classroom, you cannot expect student-led conferencing to work, or even to be taken seriously. It may take even a year or two to upgrade classroom practice. Don't expect student-led conferencing to be completely successful until students have received the training in self-assessment – it will not work.

- Understand the logistical hurdles. In elementary school, one teacher takes charge of helping students prepare their work for the conference, facilitates and supervises the event, and ensures that the experience actually benefits student learning. In junior and senior high schools, students see several teachers.

Obviously, if you have Teacher Advisors who already oversee the progress of a group of students, across all their courses, these people are ideally placed to facilitate the conferences during which the students will present evidence from all their courses. This bringing together of all the learning into one major piece of reflection and presentation is extremely useful: it shows the students themselves where the peaks and troughs in their overall performance are, and what must be done to improve their overall success.

The student will select examples of their work for their portfolio that show their best achievement, and to illustrate the difficulties they are currently having and what they need to focus on for improvement. Identifying what they need to improve is the beginning of the improvement process. With good feedback from the teacher and from fellow students, the student will understand the specific next steps they need to take to overcome the barriers to progress. In this way, the portfolio will point the way towards improvements in achievement. The role of the Teacher Advisor in schools is to provide a group of students with someone who oversees their overall learning and encourages students to reflect on their specific achievement and steps towards improvement. If your school does not have Teacher Advisors, are there other ways in which a teacher could help students in this way? In some schools, the homeroom teacher might fulfill such a role, although this would constitute a major change to what the homeroom teacher typically does. You might have to create an entirely new role, called something like "student-led conference facilitator."

This is how the process works best: The specialist subject teacher and the student, as part of their normal teaching and learning functions in the classroom, decide which items of the student's work provide the clearest indication of the student's strengths and areas for improvement. The student organizes these examples in the portfolio so that she or he can share them with some else in an intelligible and meaningful way. The student-led conference facilitator helps to oversee this process, and to organize the actual event at which the students present their portfolios to an audience – other students, parents, or other adults who are important to the student.

- Make the conference a significant event in the learning year. We would hesitate to do this more than once a year, although we would understand the argument for once a semester. We suggest the relative infrequency for a number of reasons: first, it is quite complicated to organize and is worth doing if it is done well. Second, making it an infrequent event gives it a sense of importance. Third, if you want the student to present their work to an important adult, these people will not be able to offer their time very often.

- The purpose of the conference is not just another form of reporting for each course: it is about requiring the students to be accountable for their learning. The event can be 'uncoupled' from the traditional systems of reporting, which have a different purpose. Schools will still have a responsibility to report to parents in the usual formats, grades and so on, most of which will have limited impact on the students' self-efficacy, sense of control over their own learning, or development as a responsible learner. The student-led conference is linked to the traditional reporting process but also separate from it.

- Just as the purpose of student-led conferences is different from that of normal reporting, so the audience can be different, too. Some older students will wish to present themselves and their achievement to people other than their immediate family. In some cultures, the extended family might be a more significant audience. For some students, their peers would be a more important group. For others again, the most motivating audience might be an authentic 'expert' – a professional engineer or architect, or lawyer or financier. As part of their Careers Guidance programs, schools will have contact with representatives of many careers and professions. Some employers will also be willing to mentor and advise senior students, or to be the audience for an important presentation by the student.

- There are two points of view about whether the experience should be offered as an option to students. Students who have chosen to take part will be more motivated and, therefore, probably more successful. However, offering a choice may discourage some students who would actually benefit most, and create an even wider gap between the aspiring and confident students and their more reticent counterparts. Perhaps a possible compromise would be to have annual student-led conferencing as a requirement for students, with credit attached for successful completion of certain criteria, up to grade 10, and allow choice for students above that level. At least by grade 10, students will all have had sufficient experience to determine what they want for themselves.

All our advice so far about recognizing and encouraging early progress in assessment strategies has been about getting into classrooms, watching and talking to teachers about what they are doing, and asking good questions to find out more, to encourage reflection, and to help teachers decide how to move the work forward. You are asking how these Big 5 Principles of assessment for learning (see figure 1.2) are slowly being translated into teacher action. The next section will take you out of the classroom, to where you can think more abstractly about how to make assessment for learning a permanent feature of your school, not just a one-year wonder.

Connect with Other Initiatives

Many schools and school leaders seem to have the habit of planning towards annual priorities. This year's priorities are front and centre in this year's school development plan. Sometimes, these priorities are described through the title of the initiative that drives them; for example, "Differentiated Instruction," "Feedback for Learning," "Understanding by Design," or "Curriculum Mapping." The initiative is introduced through in-service training and the three-ring binder, and then the teachers are expected to deliver. At the beginning of the following year, another capitalized initiative moves up the priority list.

External initiatives are the "spinning plates" of every school leader's nightmare. You have just managed to get all the plates spinning, each on its separate pole, and here comes another one. You have no clear criteria to discriminate among the plates and to decide which one to let fall.

If this model is even close to the way your school is conducted, changing assessment practice in the school is probably going to fail. The goal is to make assessment for learning part of the fabric of your school: the way all your learners – administrators, teachers, support staff, and students – do business. It is not an initiative to be achieved during one year under the spotlight and then replaced by something else. It is not an add-on, or an extra, or a temporary interest. We are trying to change a set of habits regarding learning and teaching, and to change those habits for good. This is as difficult as changing any other set of habits.

The external climate in which schools live is often riddled with "initiatives." Many provinces, for example, have numeracy or literacy initiatives to which districts and schools are required to give priority. Depending on the wishes and whims of Ministers of Education, work skills might suddenly appear on schools' agendas, or healthy eating, or new physical education requirements. Some of these have special funding and specific requirements from the district, the province, or jurisdiction, or even – in England, for example – the nation. School leaders are obliged to respond to these imperatives, and will often decide to adopt them into the school in the same unconnected way in which they are presented outside.

It does not have to be this way. In fact, we would argue that it should not be this way. Schools do not improve through initiatives: they improve by the identification and persistent pursuit of long-term, important goals. Temporary and fragmented initiatives must be woven into and through these long-term goals, not replace them.

Weaving your school improvement plan

The best way to envisage the difference between school goals and initiatives is through a matrix. Along one axis are the initiatives the school is trying to juggle; along the other are the underpinning strands of the long-term improvements. In-services and other school processes are driven by the strands, not by the initiatives. School leaders must plan strategically before they start to do anything, to understand the connection between initiatives and goals and to provide the confidence they need to plan for long-term improvement, not just short-term compliance.

We can illustrate this idea through constructing a notional matrix (see figure 2.1). Along one axis are the current initiatives the school is facing.

Implications for Teaching	Initiatives			
	Differentiated Instruction	Assessment for Learning	Understanding by Design	Parents as Partners
Clear learning goals	Yes	Yes	Yes	
Student-led conferences		Yes		Yes
Students choose next step		Yes		

Figure 2.1 Notional matrix.

You work across your list of initiatives, looking under the headings of each one to check the implications for what teachers will need to do. Do the same for each one, and list the implications down the vertical axis, in the boxes on the left-hand side. You will notice how the same implications appear under more than one Initative heading. This should give a clear idea of what you will have to focus on in your professional development seminars, your teacher conversations, teacher evaluations, classroom observations, and feedback processes.

Instead of having initiatives as your school goals, you will now focus on a small number of explicit developments in your teaching, as a whole school. Achievement of these goals will deliver most, if not all, of the aspects of the initiatives you feel obliged to adopt. You can find your own names for these goals: they are now clearly yours.

Some schools are so anxious about the external requirements that they begin this analysis with the external initiatives. Other schools are more confident, or more rebellious. They are determined that the change process will be driven by their priorities and values, not those imposed from outside. These schools will start with their goals, consider the implications for teaching, and only then check whether they are addressing the requirements of the programs and initiatives mandated by the district or the province.

Periodic review and adjustment

By developing your own strategic plan for improvement, you are in a better position to adapt to changing circumstances as the process unfolds. As part of the identification of your goals, you will have thought about what achievement of those goals will look like in practice. At the beginning of both this chapter and the previous one, we have offered some concrete illustrations of what you should see and hear in classrooms if the principles of assessment for learning are actually working in your school. These are what we can call the "success indicators." Developing success indicators as part of your plan will enable you to check periodically, take account of what you find, and adjust your actions accordingly.

In Stage Three, we will discuss how you evaluate assessment for learning development as part of the ongoing cycle of school self-review and improvement. At this stage, as the number of teachers involved grows and you are planning to involve others, your goal is to help teachers see how things fit together. They should realize that the success indicators for Differentiated Instruction, for example, look very similar to the success indicators for Assessment for Learning. You're not asking your teachers to do many new and unconnected things all at once, but to focus on a few aspects of their teaching that will lead to the delivery of several of the requirements.

Lead Adult Learning

In Stage One, we discussed finding the right people to lead the first wave of assessment for learning development, and the importance of understanding what these people need to help them learn new classroom strategies. The 'pioneers' in a change process are usually self-directing people: they like challenge and have the confidence to break new ground. In Stage Two, as you involve more 'settlers', the focus on them as adult learners becomes even sharper than before. As the school leader, you must consider your teachers as learners as thoroughly as you would like your teachers to consider their students. You are a learner, too: knowing how you learn best, what motivates you, and how you challenge yourself is an essential part of successful school leadership.

The Feedback for Learning project in Winnipeg was based on the premise that all the adults in a school are learners, rather than mere employees. We were determined that the principles of adult learning should be applied to all professional development strategies to ensure their effectiveness. Sometimes, this meant challenging long-established assumptions about what teachers need and deserve.

The key principles of adult learning are:

- recognition of prior experience
- flexibility regarding learning styles
- choice

The same principles apply, with others, to the learning needs of students, but with different ramifications.

Recognition of prior experience

Your understanding of the prior experiences of your colleagues may depend on where those experiences have taken place. If you or some of your teachers are new to the school, some effort may be required to discover where people have been, what they have been doing, what they have learned, and where they still need to develop their skills. You can read people's files and get only a shadow of the complex reality of their professional lives. It is necessary to ask good questions and avoid assumptions about a teacher's prior experience.

We know that many of the strategies now identified as those in assessment for learning have been around in classrooms for many years. We started teaching before the current emphasis on external curriculum requirements, testing, and accountability squeezed some of the confidence and creativity out of our teaching. Many teachers in the final stages of their careers remember the first decade of their careers and the exciting ideas they introduced into their teaching, only some of which have survived. Instead of asking whether your teachers are "doing assessment for learning," ask instead about some of the classroom strategies that come under that heading. We looked at this in Stage One: as the development spreads around the school and new people come on-board, you may need to ask again.

In order to plan for teachers' professional learning needs, you must know something about what they already do, and whether this is just intuitive or underpinned by understanding. Intuition alone is not a firm enough foundation to develop the work further. If the teacher encounters difficulties, she may tend to give up, assuming that her intuition is actually mistaken. Perseverance needs deep roots.

Recognition of prior experience includes the affective as well as the cognitive experiences. No adult learning starts with a blank slate. Even if their actual knowledge about assessment is limited, teachers have attitudes about the issue, many of them possibly negative. It is a highly emotive issue, etched deep into many of our experiences as children and adults. As you talk to teachers about their approaches to assessment, and help them to clarify the difference between assessment for learning and assessment of learning, you will hear some of these emotional reactions. Pay attention to them: these reactions reveal why some teachers find these changes so difficult, and how you can best support them.

> The word *assessment* carries such a weight of baggage that we decided in Winnipeg to avoid it altogether as part of the title of our work. We called it Feedback for Learning instead to avoid the negative connotations that attach to our experience of being on the receiving end of the process.

Some of teachers' anxieties about assessment stem from a fear that information about how well students are learning will be used to judge their effectiveness as a teacher. To some extent, of course, this is true, but we first need to understand that the prime purpose of assessment for learning is to help teachers and their students improve the students' learning and achievement. To put it simply, assessment for learning improves test scores and grades. This is the powerful message from all the research, and we must remember it all the time. There is no tension between assessment for learning strategies in the classroom and student grades: the existence of the first will lead to the enhancement of the second.

Flexibility regarding learning styles

Our understanding of different learning styles and multiple intelligences and how they affect the students' achievement is well established, but sometimes that understanding does not appear to extend to teachers as adult learners. We still offer teachers an aural, undifferentiated experience, in a bare sports hall or an anonymous hotel, and presume that all of them will learn enough to go away and act on what they hear. We are constantly astonished that anyone still believes that the mass lecture is an appropriate way to initiate learning, especially for teachers when the 'medium' is directly contrary to the 'message'.

There are many different ways to interest teachers in assessment for learning. If you are introducing an individual to the ideas, listen and watch to understand how they learn, or ask them directly and then try to adapt what you do to meet their needs. If you are organizing a staff meeting or a professional development event to introduce or reinforce assessment for learning ideas, you can respect the different learning styles quite explicitly.

In one school we worked with, the most recent focus for professional development had been identification of the four learning styles – visual, auditory, reading, and kinaesthetic – and their implications for teaching. The next professional development session was on assessment for learning. To validate and respect the learning styles information, the session was arranged so that teachers were asked to decide their own preferred learning style. The 'readers' were then asked gather in one corner, the 'visuals' in another, the auditory learners in another, and the kinaesthetic learners in another. Each group was then given an appropriate way to discover and share more about the principles of assessment for learning.

For the readers, a jigsaw exercise was provided in which some key extracts were divided up, read, and shared to construct the whole picture. The auditory people were given some statements to discuss and present; the visual learners were given paper, crayons, and other materials with which to construct a visual representation of the key points; and the kinaesthetic people chose from a range of activities, including building a human shape and creating a role play to explore and explain the main ideas. Time frames were established, the groups were given space to work without disturbing each other, and each one presented the ideas to the whole group in the style of their choosing.

That was a great session. A bit noisy, but good fun, memorable, and it consolidated their previous learning, too.

In your school, after the initial introduction of ideas in Stage One of the process, the ongoing professional development offered to teachers should be as differentiated as possible, within the constraints of time and budget. Different levels of expertise can be provided, too, within a professional development program, asking teachers to choose the level of group that suits them. Teachers new to these ideas might join a Novices group, those with more experience might be best served by a Consolidating group, and there might be a Looking for New Challenge group, too, for people interested in stretching into more uncharted territory. Some people may make poor choices, but the alternative is for someone to allocate people to a certain level, which could interfere with the very learning it was designed to promote.

Choice

Choice is fundamental to adult learning. Choice is part of what it means to be an adult; to dictate the means and circumstances of learning to an adult learner is to undermine the chance of success.

Of course, there are varying degrees of choice. In Stage One, we suggested providing choice to teachers about whether they join the change process immediately or hold back for a while. That is an example of providing choice. Another example we have just mentioned: you provide different levels of professional development and ask the teachers to join the group or the activity that best reflects their skills and confidence. The fact that some may make poor choices is actually less important than the effect of choice on the engagement of the teachers involved.

You have offered different learning pathways and made no assumptions about the printed word being the main source of information. You have encouraged people to choose when and how they become involved, but that is only in the early stages. Once assessment for learning is established as the way your school does business, a year or two down the road, then the choice for teachers may be to stay in this school or move to another. What other choices can you offer without undermining the overall direction?

You could offer people choice about their working partners. Grade-level teams, or departments, may be the natural and logical arrangement for meetings and ongoing professional development, but there could be some flexibility if necessary. If there is someone the teachers think could help them with a particular issue, try to make that person available to them. Making choices enables adult learners to feel more in control over their own learning, keeps them on track for longer, and increases the chance of deep engagement. That is what you want.

One of the Winnipeg school principals told teachers embarking on assessment for learning that, within reason and budget permitting, she would give them the resources they wanted to make their classroom strategies work. If they wanted blue folders for the students' portfolios, they got blue folders. If they wanted another chart stand to display Task, Intent, and Criteria for their students, they got another chart stand. When a teacher asks you for something, ask them how this will help improve the links in their classroom between assessment and learning. If they can explain that, provide whatever assistance you can. That is a powerful demonstration of your commitment and your willingness to help them change, too.

School leaders are learners, too. Everything we know about adult learning applies to you. You have a wealth of prior experience. We have already suggested how you refer to this to help you decide how to lead this change process in your school. You have a preferred learning style, just like everyone else. You have chosen to read this book, but there may be other ways you would prefer to learn about assessment for learning. If you know you learn best by watching someone else's practice, for example, visit a school where assessment for learning is more established, and observe how AFL has seeped into every aspect of the school's life.

We know that learners, adult and child, should reflect from time to time about what they are learning, what evidence there is of that learning, and what the next steps in learning should be. Many principals have told us how important this reflection is for them, too, and how rarely they seem to do it. There has to be a space in your day or your week when you can think quite dispassionately about what is happening around you. It could be in the shower, while you are exercising, or driving home, or you could plan for it.

Focus on motivation

We know the importance of motivation for any learner. Young children are more driven by intrinsic motivation: they learn because they want to learn. As we grow, and as schooling affects us, too, motivation can change to being largely extrinsic. Now, we learn for reward or to avoid punishment. Assessment for learning, applied to both students and their teachers, tries to push the motivation back towards the intrinsic and encourage the learner to feel more engaged in the assessment process. Intrinsically motivated learners, adult or child, will know quite a lot about their own learning through receiving regular, high-quality feedback. They will have evidence of progress over time to reassure them that effort and commitment will pay off. They will understand what is expected of them and how to be successful. These learners are going to be more engaged than before.

Of course, there will be teachers, and students, too, who will remain passive. We have been in many schools where the initial attitude of the teachers is "Just tell us what to do and we'll do it." They will comply with requirements but are not prepared to engage. If you want sustainable change in your school, you will have to work hard to change that passive compliance into more active engagement. Make sure that your teachers are clear about what is expected of them and the strategies you expect to see in their classrooms. Use every opportunity to provide positive feedback about how their practice is developing. Give teachers choices about when and how to be involved, and opportunities to learn from people they trust – often, other teachers.

Finally, let's deal with the most effective motivator for many teachers: enlightened self-interest. Consider the benefits for teachers when assessment for learning takes root in their classrooms:

- When students are clear about what is expected of them, they manage their own learning more effectively. The teacher is less frequently called upon to answer questions about "What do I do next?" and "Is this finished?"

- Coaching and encouraging students to apply criteria to their own and each other's work before the teachers sees it saves the teacher marking time. The students receive faster feedback without the teacher's needing to provide all of it.

- Students who are more engaged with their work behave better. Disruptive behaviour in the classroom is reduced. This is not a miraculous change. There will always be students who, for reasons beyond the control of the school, act out their frustrations in the classroom. But if only a small proportion of students are less of a nuisance, the teacher's day gets better and less tiring.

- Teachers feel on firmer ground when making judgments about students' achievement, and less vulnerable to students and parents questioning these judgments.

- More work is done by some of the students, to a higher standard and handed in on time, because the students take greater responsibility for their own learning. The teacher spends less time chasing incomplete work.

- The next steps chosen by the students, based on the feedback they have received and their understanding of the requirements, are more likely to be followed through than next steps decided by the teacher.

- Student grades and scores rise and make the teacher look good!

When teachers are far enough into AFL strategies to see how they are working out, ask them about the implications for themselves. Most teachers do not want to return to the way their classrooms were before. Changing the habits of assessment in the first place may seem like hard work, but once the new routines are in place, many teachers will not go back, even if there is no requirement to continue.

Achieve Teachers' Engagement

There are many ways to encourage, and retain, teachers' engagement, enthusiasm, and participation. The following will provide some suggestions.

Pay attention to staff turnover

In Winnipeg Inner City schools, staff turnover was a constant feature of school life. Sometimes, people stayed in the school but changed their assignment, which helped to spread understanding of the work around the school. But, more often than that, teachers left the school for many reasons and were replaced by others who had not encountered this work before. We had to assume that most incoming teachers into our schools knew nothing about these assessment strategies.

There are a number of steps you can take to prevent staff turnover's diluting the progress of assessment for learning in your school. First, even before joining your school, teachers should be aware of the important features of the norms and expectations in the building. At interviews, ask questions about the prospective teacher's understanding of some of the key ideas, and the information you give about the school and the position can refer to assessment for learning principles and strategies to alert newcomers to what will be expected.

Second, you will probably have printed information available for the new teacher to explain how the school works. Include in this some of the briefest and most digestible of the written resources explaining how AFL works in the school. Other teachers may offer a few examples of what they do, to make these ideas more explicit.

Third, think carefully about the team that will accommodate the new teacher, if you have any choice. Principals in Winnipeg realized that the placement of the new teacher in a team could determine the ideas and support to which that person would be exposed. The team then acted as the AFL mentor and guide to the newcomer.

Finally, remember that even teachers who have been exposed to the early in-service sessions about AFL, at Stage One, may well need a refresher. Often, teachers in Winnipeg told us that they didn't really 'get it' the first time. Only after thinking and trying new strategies for a while did they really make sense of all the ideas and research findings they had been offered right at the beginning. When you've provided the original in-service yourself, that's not what you want to hear, but we realized that this was not necessarily a fault on our part. All adult learners don't absorb information in the same way or at the same rate, and some will need to return to the basic ideas before those ideas truly make sense.

Periodically, throughout the year, spend a few minutes reminding your colleagues – and yourself – what you are trying to do and why. Why do we explain the tasks and intent at the beginning of a unit? Why is it useful for students to play a part in developing a rubric? What help do students need to decide their own next steps in learning? Why do you use "Task, Intent, Criteria" to begin a staff meeting? Gradually, through practise and repetition, the brain adopts new habits of thinking and doing, and these changes are likely to be sustained.

There was one other mechanism available to us in Winnipeg. When teachers joined the division, they were offered a series of induction sessions, and we had half a day to introduce them to the key ideas of assessment for learning and their implications for teaching. It was better than nothing, but only just! At the very start of a new assignment, teachers are often overwhelmed with new information and pay most attention to the immediate needs. The best you can do is to share one or two big ideas, a couple of classroom strategies, and the names of some people in their school on whom they can call for more help and support. The last of these is probably the most important. Pay attention to who is assigned to look after the incoming teacher in your school.

Encourage networking

The more you know about what is happening in your classrooms, the better able you are to become a vehicle for networking in your own school first. In conversation with a teacher, ask, "Have you seen what Jane is doing to develop criteria with her students? Ask her about it, and especially how she uses the chart stand. I'm sure she wouldn't mind your watching when she's doing it with the next unit. I'll sit with your students for a while if you want to go across and see. I need to talk to them anyway about their portfolios." Simple, helpful, everyone gains.

At this stage in your school, two types of teacher networking should be encouraged. The first is the in-school conversation among the teachers involved in the work, possibly including the outside supporter if you have been using one. A lunch meeting is good for this. Joining in yourself provides an efficient catch-up for you as well, or this could be the chance for your vice-principal or another member of the school leadership team to hear what's going on first-hand.

The other type of networking is between the actively involved teachers and their colleagues. The as-yet-uninvolved teachers' approaches and attitudes to change will be more diverse. There will probably be one or two people whose behaviour in adult conversation is unhelpful sometimes, and anyone trying to share might need support. Do not assume anything: if you are asking an active teacher to share their practice, check whether they want you there. If you are going to be there, what does the teacher want you to do?

Support effective teacher meetings

In Stage Two of introducing assessment for learning in your school, encouraging teachers to talk to each other about their assessment practice is crucial. More than any other factor that encourages ideas to spread around a school, teacher-to-teacher contact works best. Anne Davies says that "Change spreads like a virus," and that is exactly right, even though the image is not very attractive.

In Stage One, you will have observed how groups of teachers function, because teacher teams and their meetings are a key vehicle of sustainable change. These considerations remain very important in Stage Two, when more teachers are joining the process. Here is some advice.

- When AFL becomes a normal part of the school's activity, then it can be discussed at after-school meetings, but until then, the 'twilight slot', or late afternoon, is not the best time. People are tired and are least receptive to challenge and change. If you can find time for a team to meet during the day, they will achieve more, faster. If they are willing to meet at lunchtime, buy them lunch. If part of an in-service day can be devoted to team talk and sharing best practice, even better.

- Try to control your anxiety about what teachers talk about when you are not there. Some teachers and teams will not be affected at all by the presence of the administrator or school leader, but others will. Some teams need to be left alone. You can request oral or written feedback from the team leader.

- Speaking of team leaders … make no assumptions about the skills or confidence of a team leader. Some of the best teachers do not make good team leaders, and vice versa. Offering coaching and support to your team leaders in how to lead an effective meeting will be time well spent when meetings are so significant in the change process.

- Basic needs matter, too: a table to lean on, a comfortable chair, and a little food to eat can make all the difference to the willingness of adults to engage their brains.

- Some of the best meetings about classroom practice take place in a classroom, not the staff room. How about having some, if not all, of your staff meetings in classrooms and opening the meeting with ten minutes of "show and tell" by the teacher who is using one of the AFL strategies in that room?

Coach for learning conversations

Much of the best teacher conversation is one-on-one: two people, talking. Do we really need help with making such encounters effective in a professional environment? Yes, we think we do. Look at the types of conversation we all experience. There is the *sympathetic conversation*, where one person wants to talk and expects nothing from the listener except sympathetic responses. All you have to do is say, "Oh, I know," from time to time. Sometimes that is exactly what the tired teacher or school leader needs, but we would not call that a learning conversation. There is also the *all-about-me* style, where one person makes a comment and, almost before it is finished, another person launches into a monologue of their own. That is not a learning conversation, either.

A *learning conversation* has three distinct characteristics:

- its purpose is to help learning, not just to recount it
- it relies on helpful questions and careful listening
- it includes a consideration of outcomes and next steps

Person A asks a good question, either open-ended so that the choice of focus rests with Person B, or more focused so that Person B has a place to start. Person A then listens carefully to Person B's answer. Any questions asked by Person A must be designed to help Person B think. These questions are not just about finding out about things. They tend to be about why something was done, not just what was done. To find the most helpful questions, you have to listen very attentively, and understand what is not said as well as what is said. If you have limited time, and both people have things to offer, share the time and reverse the roles at some point so that each has the chance to benefit from the good questions of the other.

As the conversation is rounded off, the people ask each other, "What do you think is happening right now? How can you tell? What do you think you need to do next?" With practise and care, a few minutes' conversation can be really useful.

In Transactional Analysis, this is called an "adult-to-adult uncrossed transaction." An understanding of Transactional Analysis might help you to assess why conversations with some people are effective and, with others, they keep going wrong. The details of where to find more information are in the Further Reading section at the end of this book.

Encourage networking among schools

Encouraging an interest in what is happening in other schools has a number of benefits. First, it widens the available ideas and approaches at a time when teachers may have gone a little way down the road of change but got stuck and need some fresh thinking. Second, it gives people the motivation and opportunity to present what they are doing to others. Those presentations sharpen the mind and make the presenters decide what is important about what they are doing: they work for adult learners just as they do for our students. Just like younger learners, teachers can share what has not worked as well as what has been successful. They are more likely to do so if they are confident that their struggles will not be criticized. It is encouraging for new learners to hear about some of these struggles from people who have a little more experience with the strategies. A third benefit is support of future networking, as people discover others with similar challenges or similar ways of working, or just people whom they like and want to talk to again. A fourth benefit of networking is that it is often easier for teachers to talk to people from a different school about their work. A positive experience might provide the confidence they need to share more in their own school.

If you are working as part of a wider group, in the same district or division, that group should help provide a time and place for several schools to come together. If such outside encouragement is not available, ask two or three of your colleagues to join you in organizing a group. It might take a while, if you want to share an in-service day, for example, or even a staff meeting that can be spared from specific school business, but it is worth the effort to make it happen.

If you find the luxury of a shared in-service day, plan it to get the maximum benefit. If it goes well, if people have fun and learn a lot, they will want to do it again. If the little things go wrong – not enough parking space, not enough coffee, the groups are too big, or the rooms too cold – that will be all that people remember. So it is important to invest some time in the success of the venture if you're going to do it at all.

Meet with other school leaders

Of course, in your group of school leaders, everything goes smoothly every time, everyone has a positive experience, struggles are honestly shared and sympathetically received, and great professional benefit ensues; *but* there may be some groups of school leaders where this is not always the case. What we are talking about is the purpose, conduct, climate, and culture of school leaders' meetings. If these are positive and the meetings work well, they are an excellent opportunity to discuss many of the issues raised in this book. You could derive as much benefit from that discussion as teachers will derive when they meet with their peers and talk about students' learning.

We are not going to offer generic advice about developing the quality of school leaders' meetings: what we can offer is one focus for such meetings that might prove useful. It is important that the conversation is concrete; otherwise, discussing the principles of assessment for learning generates the same vague consensus as discussing motherhood and apple pie. Focus on evidence: what would be the evidence – explicit and specific – of AFL in action in your classrooms, and how would you, as the school leader, find the evidence and then act upon it? Break down the discussion into stages.

- What would you look for to know that one or two of the Big 5 Principles presented in Stage One were in place in a grade 3 classroom, or grade 6, or grade 9?

- Who would be able to gather that evidence, from whom, how, and when?

- Who should look at and analyze that evidence once it is collected?

- How can the information be used to influence the planning process, for teaching and learning, and for the school as a whole?

- Most important: How *little* evidence do we need to reach a sound conclusion and a good basis for future planning? In assessment circles, this is known as the "sufficiency question."

How to Manage Stage Two: A Summary of Advice

Here is a summary of our suggestions to help you manage Stage Two.

- Check progress. Are you ready to move on, or do you need to strengthen the foundations before you build any more?

- Manage multiple initiatives by weaving your own plan, not spinning plates.

- Begin to look for evidence of changes in learning and teaching.

- Encourage teachers' assessment for learning practices both publicly and privately.

- Remind people about the purpose and rationale for the work, and make sure teachers new to your school are clear about both.

- Encourage the spread of AFL ideas though teacher contact and conversations.

- Share and use the idea of learning conversations at all levels in the school.

- Welcome the chance to work with other schools.

- Differentiate your professional development, to enable teachers to learn in the ways that best suit them, and at a level for which they are ready.

- Begin to focus on explicit evidence in order to stay grounded in reality and to provide specific feedback about the school's progress in AFL.

FAQs at Stage Two

1. How can we be sure that our students are mature enough to handle greater responsibility for their own learning?

   The best answer is probably "try it and see." Very young children can make good decisions about their work, given the necessary coaching, language, and opportunity. As students get older, they have to 'buy in' to the opportunity. Refer to the discussion about providing students with the motivation and rationale to take responsibility. Some young people may simply refuse to take responsibility for their own progress. They do not expect to be successful and they would prefer to 'fail cool'. The school can either write these students off as self-damaging and beyond redemption, or they can take various steps to reduce the number of students who react in this way. This will necessitate establishing the expectation and skills of learning responsibility in early grades or early in the year, and sustaining them at all levels of the school. It will also entail convincing young people by any means at our disposal that they are capable of success, and proving to them that they are learning. The first purpose of portfolios is to show learners that they are learning and making progress. Sometimes students have forgotten what they couldn't do previously and we must show them the evidence. Without the conviction that progress is possible, the students' refusal to accept responsibility is understandable.

2. How much time should I give to teachers involved in assessment for learning to cope with the extra workload involved?

   We want to distinguish between different types of workload: there is 'development time', in which new strategies are worked out and practised, and 'maintenance time', when the new strategies are actually used as a matter of routine in the classroom. If you want to give teachers the incentive of more time, it must only ever be for 'development' purposes, and not much even then. New strategies are needed that do not increase the amount of time teachers spend on providing high-quality feedback for their students and on involving them in their own learning. Such strategies can be found by analyzing the time spent already on existing habits of testing, classroom assessment, and marking/grading, and then reconstructing these habits to be more effective without increasing the amount of time they take. Teachers will do assessment differently, not more of it.

Teachers should be advised to start new assessment practices with just one group at a time in junior and senior high, and with one area of learning in elementary grades. Starting new habits does take more time for a while. With practise comes greater efficiency, and then the teacher can spread the new techniques more widely.

Some development time, for a limited period, can be helpful while teachers think through the new strategies and practise them to change their habits, but, ultimately, assessment for learning is part of teaching, not an extra.

3. **My teachers are reluctant to share ideas in a full staff meeting. What should I do?**

Trying something new is a risky business for any learner, young or older. As teachers, we know that our students need a reasonably safe learning environment, protected as far as possible from any put-downs from their peers, in order to maximize their learning. Adult learners need such a safe environment, too.

Some teachers are reluctant to share their ideas and experience with others because of the behaviour of some of their peers, who – unconsciously or deliberately – undermine the validity or credibility of what a colleague may be offering, behave defensively, or even sneer at the person who is making the effort to improve their teaching.

As the school leader, you have a responsibility to support learning, whether in the classroom or the staffroom. A number of strategies are open to you.

You can make clear from the outset that teachers' learning will be respected and there will be no 'put-downs'. You can offer the 'learning teacher' guidance and practise in how to present their strategies to others and to deal with the 'nay sayers' through the quality of their presentation.

It may be that some of your teachers do not appreciate the repressive effect of their behaviour on their peers: you may have to alert them to the possibility, and seek their help in creating a positive climate for learning and exploration. You can model how you expect teachers' sharing with each other to be received and respected. As a last resort, you can see the 'nay sayers' privately and explain your expectation that they will demonstrably support others' learning, even if they are not yet to be involved themselves. What you cannot do is just accept that this part of your school's culture is unfortunately beyond your control. It is not, and your teachers deserve better.

> The answers to the quiz from page 36 are: b, c, d, f, and h are learnng objectives. If you found this a bit tricky, you will recognize the help teachers may need to make these distinctions clear, first for themselves and then for the students.

STAGE THREE
Preparing for Sustainability

Foreword

A deliberate decision was taken at the end of year 2 not to increase the number of schools participating directly in Feedback for Learning in Winnipeg Inner City. To do so could have spread our support too thinly to be effective. Using information gathered from the teachers about the choice and impact of their strategies, we compared them to the eight steps in the scaffolding for Feedback for Learning. (See the teachers' books in this series for a full description of the steps in the scaffolding.) This analysis showed us which of the steps teachers were comfortable with and which they were still avoiding. Here's what we found and what we did.

- The most frequently implemented step was designing criteria and rubrics for and with the students. The step almost universally avoided was about reflecting on learning over longer chunks of learning. We fed this finding back to the participating teachers and discussed their reluctance about this step. To support their confidence in this area, we designed some explicit guidelines for teachers to use, and the incidence of classroom reflection increased. The focus on reflection was also well served by designing whole units with teachers, with reflection activities built in.

- Anticipating the need for long-term sustainability, we began to encourage school leaders to incorporate Feedback for Learning principles and strategies into their own work. For example, we asked them to use the language of Task, Intent, Criteria in their introductions of staff meetings and in-service. We also encouraged school leaders to adopt high-quality feedback practice when doing evaluations with their teachers.

- Finally, and in pursuit of a deeper level of learning and confidence for some of the teachers, we explored opportunities for teachers to provide professional development for each other, and to present their "work in progress" at various events and conferences.

We have incorporated these refinements into this book.

I revisited a school a year or two after my work with them, which had lasted on and off over three years, was finished. The principal was pleased to see me, but had been called out of school to a meeting. "Just make yourself at home," he said. "Go and visit some classrooms. There are some new teachers on staff who may not know who you are, but that's okay. They're a friendly bunch." In one of the classrooms the teacher was new to the school since I had worked there. I heard her explain the task and intent of the work the students were beginning. I heard her answer a student's question with another question, to encourage the student to figure out the answer for himself. I saw the poster on the wall about "Strategies: what to do when we get stuck."

During a lull, I talked to the teacher. "You obviously know all about Feedback for Learning," I said, confident that she would rattle off the eight steps and explain how she had implemented them in her room. "Feedback for what?" she said. "The task and intent, you talked about that," I insisted, trying to trigger her realization of what I was talking about. "Oh, that," she said. "That's just what we do here. I'm not sure why. Doesn't everybody do that?"

Her unconscious acceptance of Feedback for Learning strategies made me both pleased and anxious. Clearly, in this school, the ideas we had worked on together had been so well absorbed into the way the school did business that they were now the norm. But it was also clear that this newcomer knew very little about why these strategies were in place and the difference they could make to students' learning. For her, they were classroom techniques that seemed to work, so she used them. Her approach was pragmatic and uncritical, but was that enough to sustain her into an unpredictable future?

In conversation later with the principal, we talked about the roots of sustainability and the need to remind people from time to time not only about the strategies, but also about where they come from and why they work. If the quality of feedback and learning is to be sustained, the teachers will need to reflect on what they're doing, adjust it, develop it, and add to their own learning as well as the students'. Without that continual refreshment, any teaching strategies will lose their edge and insight over time, as the original understanding fades and the original instigators move on.

Task, Intent, and Criteria

In Stage Three, we run the risk of becoming embroiled in the current flurry of definitions and models of sustainability. In an effort to avoid this, our task here is to explain how each aspect of the school can be reviewed to absorb the principles of assessment for learning; to encourage you to find a sustainable balance among the values your school professes, the external conditions that surround it, and its standard operating procedures; and to consider briefly the influence of the school district on how assessment for learning can be embedded in schools.

Suggestions for Sustainability

In stages One and Two, you have been preparing the foundations of improved classroom assessment in your school and starting to build the structure. The following is a brief review.

In Stage One

- Do your homework: you must know about the basic principles of assessment and their implications. These principles all spring directly from a sound research base. The body of evidence about the impact of assessment for learning on student achievement is impressive, deep, and expanding all the time.

- Know your starting point: assessment for learning strategies are not new and you and your teachers should find out what is happening already and build from there.

- Learn from past experience of changing classroom practice: if there have been difficulties or roadblocks before, do not repeat them this time.

- Connect assessment for learning with other improvements in teaching practice you may have been working on previously.

- Think carefully about who will be actively involved in implementing AFL ideas in the first wave of change, and how you're going to encourage those people. Plan how you will keep the rest of the school in touch with what the first-wave people are doing.

- Make the best use you can of any external support available to you.

- Gradually expand the number of teachers involved, by teacher-to-teacher contact, if possible.

- Be prepared to change your own practice to model the language and strategies of AFL.

In Stage Two

- Look for signs of progress and give teachers good feedback.

- Develop a long-term strategic plan to see how all the pieces of change fit together, and start to look for specific evidence that indicates how things are going and what to focus on next.

- Focus on your teachers, and yourself, as adult learners, and raise motivation as well as skills.

- Create structures for teacher contact and conversation that will spread and deepen the understanding of AFL, including learning conversations at all levels of the school.

- Identify the evidence of AFL in action, and start looking for it in classrooms and around the school.

- Work with other schools to support and ask good questions of each other.

Many schools embarking on assessment for learning have various supports available to them in the form of people and external expertise. Part of moving towards sustainability is coming to terms with the withdrawal of these external supports. Most change processes are vulnerable at the point when the extra money or the external support runs out. In Winnipeg, we recognized this challenge a full year before it happened. If you can think ahead that far, we strongly suggest you do the same.

Once you believe that the ideas of assessment for learning have begun to spread around the school and are beginning to take root, you are in a position to plan quite deliberately for long-term sustainability. This will mean reconsidering many of the basic habits of your teachers, your school, and yourself, and changing most of those to sustain assessment for learning.

Sustaining is more than maintaining

Some schools have 'golden ages' when everything comes together and resonates perfectly with the spirit of the times and with the needs of the community. Being part of a school at such times is a privilege and a pleasure: no wonder people try to hang on to how things were. Schools do not stand still or stand alone. They are dynamic organizations, evolving naturally and as part of a larger landscape that is also evolving, sometimes slowly, sometimes faster. The school has to keep moving forward, adapting and growing, or it loses the vitality and connections that made it work so well in the past.

> *Sustainability* does not mean establishing new ways of working and then retaining those ways of working for as long as you can. Sustainability means embedding the new ways of working into the fabric of the school, a flexible fabric that will stretch to fit new circumstances. The most important principles will be sustained, but the strategies through which we realize these principles will change.

Planning for Sustainability

In reality, not many school leaders think about sustainability in the very logical and ordered way we are going to describe in the next few pages. Maybe that is because the day job is so busy that they rarely have time to step back and think about long-term things. The Winnipeg administrators we worked with, leading busy schools in a challenging inner-city environment, rarely had time during the school day to step back and see the strategic overview. We met together, of course, and discussed the more abstract implications of long-term change, but even those oases of reflection were too short to allow for the dispassionate thoughts and calm planning that we are about to suggest to you. That was an important Winnipeg lesson: time to think is hard to find and essential for sustained development.

Even when you find the time, you also need some structures to frame your thinking, or the complexities may appear overwhelming. There are many theories and books about sustainable change but not much practical help. The task is to analyze the way the school works, and see how assessment for learning can be embedded in – not just added on to – these ways of working. If you have followed stages One and Two, you will already have been thinking about changing the way your school does business, not all at once, but little by little. The following separate elements should all support each other to ensure that the AFL change is sustained in the school and old habits do not quickly reassert themselves.

The pertinent elements of a school's operation are:

1. the school's values, aims, goals, or mission statement – what it stands for and how that is expressed

2. the roles and responsibilities of various people in the school – teachers, team leaders, and support staff

3. the kinds of meetings the school has, and the professional development program it provides to develop the skills and capabilities of the adult learners

4. the school's approach to, and guidelines about, fundamental activities such as planning, marking, and classroom management

5. the systems the school has for record keeping, reporting, and parent-teacher interviews

6. the evidence you look for to illustrate that your strategies are in place and effective

7. the requirements and support that influence the school from outside, from the school district, the province or state, or from national expectations: how do we manage these external influences, which may be helpful or troublesome?

First we will look at the implications of assessment for learning for each of these parts. Then we'll see how the various parts can be kept in balance. Nothing ever stands still. Sustaining doesn't mean maintaining, but adjustment to meet changing circumstances.

Statement of values

Every school has its own statement of values and beliefs. These values are the "soul" of the school. They must be reflected in the way the school does business. They must recognize and reflect the community that the school serves. Assessment for learning, as we have seen, will mean a shift in the fundamentals of learning and teaching in the school. This fact will influence what you say in your expression of values. It should also influence how the statement of values is developed and shared. Assessment for learning applies to adult learners – teachers and school leaders – as well as the students. That fact should also be reflected in the way the school presents itself.

The school's strategic plan, action plan, improvement plan, or whatever you want to call it, is another statement of intent, which should provide the overall direction for the school, connecting the school's values and goals with the operational detail. The process by which you develop this plan with your staff will reflect assessment for learning principles: Task, Intent, Criteria are the starting points, yet again. Adult learners, like their younger counterparts, will be involved in reflecting on past performance and establishing next steps. They will also be involved in gathering and analyzing evidence of how the plan is working. School leaders could do all this themselves, but sharing the tasks will help get them done, and involving more people means the next steps are more likely to be realistic and achievable.

Roles and responsibilities

All of us in school have defined roles and responsibilities. These job descriptions should reflect the shift toward assessment for learning as a whole-school goal. We are all adult learners. We deserve the same clarity of expectations as we want teachers to provide for their students.

Therefore, we must be quite explicit about the expectations for teachers. If we want them, for example, to clarify learning outcomes and success criteria and to share them with students, we should say so. If 'learning portfolios' are to be developed, that requires specific instructions, too.

Anyone carrying an extra responsibility should know what's expected of them. Team leaders should know how often they are expected to meet with their teams, and that a record of the decisions made should be given to yourself or the vice-principal. We cannot blame anyone for their failure to meet our expectations if we have not made those expectations clear.

We have seen many job descriptions that have page after page of "activities to be undertaken." After page 1, you might lose the will to live. Even at the very end, several pages later, comes the catch-all phrase "All other activities as determined by the Principal." How much better instead to itemize the key responsibilities of the person, state a few bottom-line requirements, and then leave the person some freedom to decide how exactly they will fulfill their responsibilities. Of course, much will depend on the capability and commitment of whomever you're dealing with and you'll need to differentiate the development plan for different people in the same way that a good teacher will differentiate their approaches to different students.

Teachers' meetings and professional development

In Stage Two, we suggested a review of how teachers' meetings and professional development can be used to spread and deepen the school's understanding of AFL and how it works in the classroom. Now that you've established structures of meeting and conversations that will support AFL, consider how to sustain both the language and the strategies of assessment for learning in the longer term.

- Continue to use the language yourself, Task, Intent, Criteria, at the start of staff meetings and in-service events. Little by little, it will seep into the fabric of the school.

- Make AFL reports and feedback a standing item on staff and team meeting agendas until it is embedded into your standard practice.

- Find creative opportunities for professional development: teachers visiting each other's classrooms is probably more effective than yet another meeting. Visiting another school and bringing back ideas to share with colleagues is great professional development for teachers or for yourself.

- When you have established good working relationships with other schools who are also developing AFL, gather evidence in each other's schools. Interview a sample of each other's students. This generates good evidence, and everyone learns a great deal about the impact of AFL on the experience and motivation of students.

Guidelines about fundamental activities

Most schools have some common guidelines to encourage consistency among teachers and teaching across the school. Uniformity – that is, exactly the same teaching techniques in every classroom – would probably be too oppressive for the teacher and too boring for the learners. Consistency is different: it means that all the teachers try in their own ways to work within a shared framework of beliefs about learning and about what makes learners successful. We all agree that involving the learner in the assessment process is our aim, and we follow through with methods of doing so, appropriate to the age of the learner, the subject matter, and the circumstances. Our techniques may be different, but our goals are the same.

Your school should have some clear guidelines about the fundamental activities of teaching. For example, if teachers are expected to distinguish in their plans between learning objectives and student activities, that should be articulated in a guideline. Better still, offer a format for planning that includes this distinction, to make it easier to remember, and eventually the procedure will become a habit.

Your school should also have a School Guide to Marking for Learning. By this, we do not just mean an agreed mechanism for calculating marks or deriving grades. That is important, but it may have very little to do with the link between marking and improved learning. Many schools will need two sets of guidelines, one about assessment *of* learning (calculating marks, etc.) and one about assessment *for* learning, suggesting or recommending approaches to marking that are specifically designed to improve the students' work and to encourage them to take responsibility. If assessment for learning is going to be sustained in your school, your guidelines on any of these issues must reflect your school's expectations.

These guidelines are very useful for people new to your school, including classroom support people who have to understand the questioning techniques in use in classrooms, so that they can reinforce them in their own practice. New teachers will have instant access to information about your school's expectations. A substitute or cover teacher will also be able to see quickly the kinds of classroom assessment activities students are used to and expect.

Systems of record keeping and reporting

It may seem strange to have left such a fundamental issue as how teachers keep records and write reports to this stage. Surely you will have been thinking about this at the earlier stages? Of course, but thinking about it is not the same as arriving at definite conclusions about changes to the basic school systems. As teachers develop AFL in their classrooms, they inevitably start to amend the methods of keeping track of students' work and progress. It will be one of the things you notice as you check for progress in Stage Two. But until all teachers are involved, it is difficult to change the processes that will apply to everyone.

At this stage, or earlier, depending on the response to using AFL strategies during Stage Two, look at all the different amendments teachers have been making to their record keeping and find a consistent way forward that incorporates the characteristics of AFL. For example, you will expect that teachers' records will now capture more than just marks or scores. They will have been using more specific criteria in their marking and this will also appear in their records.

It is also important at this stage to accept that some of the teachers' information about students' learning and progress should accessible to students, and some will be recorded by the students. 'High-stake' information that will generate an important grade or score will be kept by the teacher, but students can and should keep track of the assignments they've completed, the feedback they received, the next steps agreed upon at the time, and how those next steps were turned into improvement. Teachers can help design these student records only when they have had some experience of the AFL principles at work.

Finally, when you are updating record-keeping processes to take account of new approaches to assessment, let some, if not all, of your old systems go. We can get so attached to old habits that we hesitate to let them go even when they're clearly obsolete.

Here is an example of how a slight change in the teacher's approach can make a considerable difference to the engagement of the students. In a grade 6 classroom, the teacher was encouraging students to come to terms with the idea of 'credit' that they would soon encounter in junior high. He explained what the students needed to achieve to earn a credit and then developed an Excel spreadsheet of tasks, assignments, and other assessment events on which to record the students' marks and the accumulating total as the weeks went by. Students were able to see what they had already achieved, what was still to come, how different activities were weighted, and what they needed to do to be successful. All the information was stored on the teacher's laptop in the classroom, and students regularly checked it under his supervision.

Reporting to Parents

Most school districts in North America mandate the format of the parental report, although this is not the case in schools elsewhere – in the UK and New Zealand, for example, where schools design their own. Sometimes, these report formats lag behind schools' best practice. During this transitional phase, schools may need to find a way of incorporating AFL principles into their reports without creating greater workloads for the teachers, as specific reporting may involve more words than old-fashioned reporting merely by numbers or grades.

For example, here is one change to the reports format you could make immediately. Instead of that catch-all word *Comments* that we see routinely on the bottom of a report form, change it to *Specific Next Steps* and ask teachers to include one or two, no more, next steps that would lead to an immediate improvement in the student's work. "Work harder" is not a next step. "Remember to use a new paragraph for a new idea" is a next step. Changing the heading will not necessarily change what teachers write under the heading; some further coaching and practice will be required, too, but just that one action can change the purpose of the report from being just reporting *of* learning to reporting *for* learning.

Another essential step to improve the quality of parental reporting is to reduce the frequency. Frequent reporting may be a cultural expectation and therefore very hard to shift, but it inhibits the quality of the information and its usefulness in enhancing standards. Making the student's effort dependent on the intervention of the parent is counter-productive. Only the student can improve his or her own learning: it is the student who must be well-informed and committed to improvement. If frequent reporting to parents diverts the teacher's attention from classroom learning and the students' need for good feedback, then we have truly subverted school improvement.

Student Self-Reporting

Having the students write an overall report on their own learning, progress, difficulties, and next steps at least once a year, as part of the overall report, is one approach to embedding AFL in the reporting process. The students will require writing frames and practise to make this work, but they can do it, and it is best to start as students as young as possible. Self-presentation is commonplace in adult learning and work environments; it makes sense to develop this habit in elementary school and continue it right through into senior high. Using electronic means to present learning is also essential where the school's resources allow for it: an electronic portfolio of evidence of learning containing photos and video clips as well as paper evidence and marks provides a much more comprehensive and important picture of the learner than the marks and grades alone.

Conferencing and Parents' Meetings

In Stage Two, we suggested that if your school already does student-led conferences (SLCs), part of your progress check would be to ask some questions about how they work and whether they reflect the principles of student involvement and learning improvement towards which we are aiming. If your school has not yet recognized SLCs as a natural extension of increasing the student's responsibility for their own learning, consider it now. Many schools have good experience from which you can learn. For elementary schools, Anne Davies et al.'s book *Together Is Better* will provide all the insights and practical suggestions you will need.

In junior and senior high schools, the logistics of student-led conferencing are potentially more complicated, but the need to involve the students in critique and presentation is even more crucial. At this stage in their learning lives, it is essential for students to take responsibility for their own learning: very soon they will be out in the working world. We cannot let them leave full-time education without several years' practice in how to manage, critique, correct, and present their own learning.

In Stage Two, we suggested that SLCs be considered at junior and senior high school levels, not as a continuance of elementary practice but with a rationale and style that suit the age group.

Gathering evidence

At Stage Two, we talked about developing a strategic plan that weaves together the initiatives and priorities that the school is trying to manage simultaneously. We suggested you focus on those classroom activities that are common to more than one of the school's goals, rather than trying to plan different activities to satisfy different goals. Looking for the evidence of these chosen classroom strategies has a number of useful functions.

First, looking for evidence provides you with feedback about how your chosen strategies are actually working. You will check a number of sources to find out what is happening: teachers will show you their plans and report on how their classroom activities appear to be generating better learning for their students; the students' work will show improvement in standards; the students themselves will tell you how their better understanding of the teachers' expectations leads them to be more successful.

Second, this feedback will help teachers to adjust their activities to make them even more effective. Of course, this presupposes that the teachers are provided with good feedback and encouraged to act upon it. If they are left in the dark, or are made to feel inadequate by the feedback, they lapse into resentment or even give up. The main thing the principal must do, having found some useful feedback, is to offer it to the teachers in such a way that they are encouraged to persevere. Better still, if the teachers are themselves involved in gathering and analyzing the evidence of their own activity, they are more interested in the outcomes and more likely to act upon them.

Third, the exercise of looking for, analyzing, and acting upon the evidence is what we want the teachers to be doing for, and with, their students. If we follow the same principles as we wish to apply to classroom assessment, then we can model the best practice and reinforce what we want to see happening in the classroom. Feedback for learning is a multi-level process: the teacher provides feedback for her students, and the principal ensures that the school's self-review process provides feedback for the teachers, and him/herself too. The same principles apply and the school becomes truly a learning organization.

External requirements and support

This is the last of the aspects of the school to be looked at in terms of improving the sustainability of the changes AFL could bring about in your school. What happens outside the school, at other levels of the education system, will, of course, have a major bearing on the school. If, for example, your school district has mandated the introduction of student-led conferences, this expectation might have been your first consideration, to meet the external requirement. Similarly, if an external source was offering specific grants or other encouragement to develop electronic student portfolios, this might have prompted the school to act in this direction. Conversely, your school might want to improve the quality of reports to parents by reducing the frequency, but you are prevented from doing so by the reporting regulations in your district. Or, your efforts to enhance assessment for learning in grade 8 are thwarted by the dominance of a new province-wide literacy test that distracts teachers' attention from more useful literacy improvement strategies and drives them into giving far too many practice tests. We could find endless examples of the influence of external change on internal practice, both negative and positive.

Here are a few suggestions about how to deal with an external climate that does not appear to support assessment for learning as a major focus in your school.

- Examine the details of any unhelpful external requirements and see what you can salvage. If something is not specifically prohibited, you can probably do it. If something is required, much depends on how it is done, not just whether it is done.

- Be as bold as you can manage. Your goal is to raise student achievement, progress, and preparedness for a successful learning life, and that is surely what every politician, trustee, superintendent, and parent also wants. They may not have thought about your proposed strategy for achieving these goals, so tell them as clearly as you can, with an irresistible combination of evidence and passion.

- Do as much as you can in your own school to involve the students in classroom assessment and learning, and enable them to explain to their parents what they are doing and why they are doing it.

- Use any professional networks available to you to share your conviction that assessment for learning has positive potential for all our students.

If the external climate provides positive opportunities for development of AFL in your school, the situation is more straightforward, although you may still have decisions to make. In our work in Winnipeg, school leaders were given the choice of when and how to involve the school and the teachers. Making those decisions requires you to understand the way change will happen in your school, your readiness for change, and how best to support it.

Find the Balance: Sustain the Change

So far we have considered aspects of a school's operation, one at a time. Obviously, these aspects connect with one another. When changes occur in one aspect, it will affect the others, like the vibrations caused within a spider's web when one part of the web is disturbed.

Here are some changes that will occur from time to time, over which you will have no control:

- The key person you have been relying on to coordinate the development has learned so much from doing so that he has been promoted to leadership in another school.

- Your enrolment has risen, or dropped, requiring a different allocation of resources, changes in class size, and composition.

- Three newly qualified teachers arrive in your school who are – hallelujah – knowledgeable and enthusiastic about developing AFL strategies with their students, and you will have to find a role for them.

- A change of superintendent has brought a change of district priorities and AFL has dropped down the list.

- The local newspaper describes student self- and peer assessment as evidence of teachers abdicating their responsibilities and you are swamped with anxious inquiries from parents.

To accommodate these changes, you will need to consider how they will affect the sustainability balance you have been striving to achieve. You need to stand back and see the whole spider's web of your school, all at once, and make the adjustments that may be necessary. The departure of a key person, for example, will necessitate the reallocation of some roles and responsibilities to plug the gap. The arrival of new talent provides an opportunity for changing the focus or composition of some of your teams to maximize the positive potential. You are thinking all the time about how to maintain the school's values by adjusting to ever-changing circumstances.

The easiest way to visualize this need for balance is to think of your school as a three-legged stool. The three legs are:

1. the school's values and goals

2. the school's external circumstances and pressures

3. the school's people and operational systems

If you don't pay attention to all three legs, the stool will wobble. If too much emphasis is placed on one or two of the legs, and the third is neglected entirely, the stool falls over.

The key to sustainability is to keep that image in your mind and take the time you need to see the school as a whole from time to time. That's not easy when the 'day job' is so busy and clogged with details. Maintaining the balance is one task school leaders can help each other with, if the climate of conversation and support among them is as helpful as it needs to be.

Here is an example of the balance you should seek among the three elements: the school's values; the external climate; and the way the school does business.

- In your school's values, you state the importance of involving students as active participants in their own learning.

- The external climate will include certain requirements about reporting: you have not flouted these, just added to them in keeping with your school's beliefs about learning.

- In your school's reporting process, you have deliberately included the student reflection leading to a statement by the student of their key achievements and areas for improvement.

You could pick another issue and check for the compatibility between your school's values, recognition of the external climate, and your practice. It is useful to do this from time to time, as the external climate can change and the school may need to adjust its procedures without sacrificing its beliefs.

Sustainability at the district level

If you are working at the district level, connect the advice for school leaders with current practice in your schools. Recognize that assessment for learning is a multi-layered process, starting from the premise that we are all learners and that the AFL principles apply to all of us. Our working with Winnipeg Inner City District was helped immeasurably by the superintendent's passion for the work and understanding of how it influences all layers of the school system.

This is a book for school leaders, but their effectiveness is much influenced by the school district, especially in North America. (In England, the powers of school districts, known as "Local Authorities," have dramatically decreased over the past 20 years, and in New Zealand there are no such bodies at all.) To those in positions of influence in school districts, our advice would be:

- Understand the principles of assessment for learning, their provenance, and their implications for teachers and school leadership.

- Recognize that school leaders need support and encouragement to look at school change as an explicit issue, with assessment for learning as the context for their analysis of how change works.

- Recruit, select, and train school leaders with the capability and energy to lead sustainable improvement in learning and teaching, not just to manage the status quo.

- Leave school leaders in place long enough to effect change and see it through: probably five years at least, with some performance review midway. The three stages of assessment for learning development discussed in this book roughly correspond to three years in the life of a school. It makes no sense to replace a leader in the middle of such an important change in the approach to learning and teaching.

- Encourage school leaders, consultants, support teachers, and teachers themselves to look regularly for evidence of what difference the new strategies make to student learning, progress, and measurable outcomes. These measurable outcomes will include information about student attendance, progression, dropout rates, parental involvement rates, and test scores for different groups of students. This information is the explicit feedback adult learners need to adjust their activities and be more effective. You will have started looking for evidence of impact soon after the AFL changes are introduced, but the long-term evidence is not apparent right away.

- Do not use large and temporary increase in resources to schools as a quick fix. Schools may develop processes that depend on these increased resources and then just discontinue the new practice when the temporary resources are withdrawn.

- Remain focused on transforming assessment practices as a central plank in the improvement of student outcomes.

- Model assessment for learning strategies yourself whenever you can.

How to Manage Stage Three: A Summary of Advice

The following is a summary of our suggestions for planning for, and achieving, sustainability for assessment in your school.

- Analyze the aspects of the school that must be held in balance: the school's values, the way the school does business, and the external circumstances.

- Don't rush: your school's standard operating procedures have a tenacious hold on what happens, and changing these will take some time. If you do not change them, old habits will reassert themselves as soon as the spotlight moves on to another initiative.

- Do not let the external climate so dominate your thinking that you dare not take any risks at all. Risk is part of learning. We know that successful schools are learning organizations: successful school leaders must be prepared to take risks and must encourage their teachers to do the same.

- Develop an approach to evidence-driven school action planning that will keep taking the school's processes forward.

- Assessment for learning will affect the behaviour of learners at all the layers in the system: teachers, school leaders, and district leaders. The more connected these layers can be, the more sustainable the changes they will make together.

- Remember the three-legged stool and pay attention to the balance of the school's values, its external pressures, and its people and operational systems.

FAQs at Stage Three

1. Our statement of values seems too vague. How can we make it simpler and more meaningful?

Sometimes, when you're trying to create a statement about the school's approach to assessment as a guide to teachers or parents, it reads like jargon and euphemisms strung together into sentences. We suggest the following to create something more meaningful.

After you've completed some research about assessment for learning or have analyzed your existing practice, arrange your staff into small groups, mixed by experience, approach, and specialist subject. Then proceed with the following:

a) Develop six to eight agreed-upon statements to finish this sentence: "Assessment in your school should ..." No jargon is allowed. Language must be as plain as possible.

b) For each of these statements, identify how you will know that the statement had been achieved. These are called your "indicators." Be as explicit as possible, and choose only one or two indicators for each statement.

c) Refine the original statements if necessary.

d) Write the statements and indicators on large pieces of paper and post them so that everyone can read each other's. Look for commonalities and check that nothing really important has been left out.

e) Select someone to synthesize all the statements and indicators into one set of statements and one list of indicators, using the frequency of mention as the guide to importance.

f) Publish these as the first draft, ask for refinement if necessary, then share the final version with all interested parties. The explicitness and the concrete indicators will be helpful to all those who need to use or understand the statement.

g) Use the indicators to guide your search for evidence later, when you want to check whether your assessment intentions are actually working.

2. **We've had some extra money for professional development and cover for teachers' conferencing with students. What do we do when the money runs out?**

Several months before the money is due to run out, you have some decisions to make as a school. You could put all your energy into lobbying for the extra money to continue, but that will only be a temporary solution to your problem. Or you could just shrug and settle for the expectation that the new work will fade away and people fall back into their old habits. If you want the work to be sustained, start planning for sustainability weeks, if not months, before the reduction in resources actually happens.

Form a group representing those who will ultimately keep the work going and discuss all the operational details of sustainable change. Exhortations will not be enough. Only teachers can change their teaching habits and their voices must be heard. Compromise may be required to enable teachers to take the changes step-by-step rather than all at once, as long as the impetus is maintained.

Begin the conversation with a discussion of the benefits to teachers to allow the changes to continue. Very few teachers who have experienced classrooms where assessment for learning really works will want to go back to their previous practice. They realize that having students who are more motivated, more focused, more independent, and more successful makes the teacher's day easier. Enlightened self-interest is a powerful motivator.

Students should also be reminded of the benefits to them. We should listen carefully to the students' views about what helps them learn effectively, and act on what they tell us. If possible, use video or audio to capture the students' words, and make the tapes available for teachers to watch and listen if they choose. The actual student voice carries a powerful message, more powerful than other forms of 'student voice' data.

One project several years ago involved improving the experience of students moving from junior high into senior high school. We commissioned a researcher to gather information from the students themselves. During a tense meeting with senior high teachers, she played some snippets of what the students had said. Instantly, silence fell as the teachers listened. The silence continued when the tape stopped. They were thinking. No miraculous changes happened but the tide had turned and space had been created for new habits to be formed. Remembering this reminds us that habits learned through the limbic brain can only be changed through the limbic brain, through experience and emotion, not just reason and intellect.

3. **Our parents still insist on grades on reports. Do we have to provide them?**

Parents need and deserve to know as much as we can tell them about our efforts to increase the emphasis on assessment for learning and to keep it distinct from assessment of learning. As we said at the beginning, these two are not better or worse, they are different. What matters is the purpose. If the purpose of reporting is just to inform parents about achievement and progress, as simply as possible, then we can use a grade. That will not tell the parent – or the student – anything about what the grade represents, or how it could be improved. If we want reporting to actually improve the student's performance, rather than just to measure it, then using grades and not much else will not help at all. Parents cannot improve a student's grades, and neither can teachers. Only learners can improve their learning.

An additional consideration is how long it takes teachers every year to complete every set of reports to parents, and how many times a year this will be done. Some of those hours could be spent on activities such as planning and effective feedback that will have a far greater impact on the quality of the students' results.

Once a school is clear about how assessment for learning can positively influence academic results, and has suggestions about how reporting to parents could be adjusted to resonate with AFL principles, then the discussions should start.

If the format and frequency of reports are determined by the district, not the individual school, then the debate should occur at that level.

4. Will assessment for learning be made mandatory?

In England, assessment for learning strategies are already embedded in the accountability frameworks for both teachers and schools. You cannot make something legally binding if you do not have the power to monitor it. Assessment for learning is quite hard to 'check' in this way: to do so you would have to be in the classroom, listening and watching, so that you can see *how* teaching, learning, assessment, and feedback are being handled. Schools have the capacity to do this, through teacher evaluation procedures and other accountability processes, but it would be harder to make classroom strategies mandatory at other levels. When so much depends on the habits of mind of both teachers and students, it is probably more effective for change to happen because people are convinced that it will benefit them, rather than because they are required to change.

EPILOGUE

The first phase of our work in *Feedback for Learning* (FFL) ran from 2000 to
2003. Since that time, we have continued to extend the ideas and procedures
developed in the first three years. Today, all 21 Inner City schools are involved in
FFL; 10 schools have been involved in the three-year project described in these
documents, but all school leaders in the 21 schools have been participating in the
Conversations about Feedback for Learning since the beginning. As a group of
schools, we are convinced that we are on the right track. We see more awareness
and understanding from our staff and the leadership of the schools of the
importance of FFL for our students, but most significant of all is that the students
themselves are telling us and showing us what they need to become independent
learners. Based on this, we are able to use the scaffolding steps to involve the
students in their learning more effectively than we were doing.

Teacher training

We have used a combination of in-servicing, small study groups, and classroom
visits, which gives the most effective framework for changing teacher practice.
We have built and are extending strong internal supports, including integrating
Feedback for Learning in all our work through our district support staff (Kathy
Collis/Thompson Owens), but still use external supports as "check-in" points.
For example, Caren Cameron, an educational consultant from British Columbia,
comes twice a year to work with our school staff leaders and Ruth Sutton
continues her connection with us.

School leadership – responsibility and understanding

The development of our school leaders is an important facet of sustaining change. Our District Continuing Conversations focus on the identification and collection of classroom evidence of the implementation of Feedback for Learning. The main questions are, How do we, as school leaders, know what is really happening in classrooms? Do we talk purposefully to students ourselves? Do we structure risk-free conversations with our staff? What kind of evidence is the most valuable to collect? What do we do with this information? School administrators are spending more time in classrooms observing and talking to the students. They are focusing initially on the area of 'task and intent' as outlined in the scaffolding; i.e. are the teachers establishing a clear context for learning and do the students know what they're doing and why? The scaffolding is the framework for the school leaders' observations.

Our school leaders also collect formal data through the Comprehensive Assessment Program, the Grade 8 Assessment, and other test results.

Share discussion/common language expectations

Together, the school leaders, support staff, and superintendent developed our shared vision for the work of our schools. An integral piece of this is the development of a common language to ensure that collectively we work together. Fifteen years ago we developed Principles of Learning and Assessment based on curricula outcomes to provide the Inner City schools staff with a common language. We have now reworked the Principles to include what we have learned from Feedback for Learning. We continue the search for concrete examples of Feedback for Learning scaffolding to develop our own understanding.

Organizational structure

We have formed 'clusters' of schools within the district (five at elementary, two at secondary, with three schools in each) to facilitate collegial discussions across schools among school leaders and staff. A key component of the cluster is the Learning Support Teacher in each cluster, who acts as a local internal resource to the staff of the three schools. The Learning Support Teacher works in classrooms, modelling appropriate strategies. They are trained by the district support staff.

Role of superintendent

The role of the superintendent is critical in the effectiveness of this work. The superintendent provides a framework that expects the focus of the school's work to be on improving students' learning, despite all the other needs/pressures in schools. The framework establishes priorities; expects school leaders to be actively engaged in understanding the strategies and approaches being introduced; facilitates the involvement of staff; and illustrates how successful classrooms should look and sound. The development of a climate of trust between the school leaders, support staff, and superintendent involved in this work is a necessary underpinning for the open discussions on where we are and what we do next.

The superintendent has active involvement in the discussion, plans, and commitments, yet makes no assumptions about implementation. Initially, schools were given a choice as to whether they would be involved in FFL, but it was made clear that eventually all schools would be involved.

As the leadership of the district, the school leaders and I found a practical, organizational way of providing ongoing support within *existing* budgets and staffing allocations. Together, we ensured that this work receives the support it needs to flourish. We had realized it was important to plan for sustainability from the beginning, which meant that we could not use a project or additional grant funding. Therefore, we decided to use staffing from the allocation of positions given annually to the Inner City District and took the staff time for Ruth Sutton, Thompson Owens, and Kathy Collis "off-the-top." In effect, the schools agreed to have fewer positions available for their school staffing. Professional Development funds were also allocated out of existing budgets. The decisions were made by the Inner City District Staffing Committee and Curriculum & Assessment Committee.

Other factors

A large part of the success of our work in FFL was due to the fact that this program was part of a more long-term process of change started 15 years ago. We had already set in place many procedures that enhanced the work of FFL; for example, the Inner City Arts Training program, which started 16 years ago.

Our Inner City Arts Training Program provided a model for ongoing teacher development, which could be applied to our FFL work. This model showed us that in order to have successful, sustainable change in teacher practice, we had to provide ongoing opportunities for learning, including in-classroom practise of new strategies, followed by reflection and discussion with peers. The Inner City Arts Training Program is structured with staff attending three professional development days spread through the year and following up each session by applying and using the strategies they have learned to their work in their classrooms. The teachers keep reflective journals and return to the next professional development session ready to share their experiences with their colleagues. This cycle continues throughout the year, with the training leaders visiting the participant's classroom to provide feedback to teachers in the 'real' setting. In the FFL work, the District Support Staff and the Learning Support Teachers work in the classrooms side-by-side with the teachers.

Conclusion

There are continuing challenges in our work with FFL, such as staff turnover and the requirement of continuous staff development. We cannot rely on untrained teachers knowing even the basics of effective assessment and feedback practices. We are building teacher leadership across the district to spread the understanding and support. In the future, as we continue the focus on Feedback for Learning, we must persevere and sustain the change process. It is still evolving.

We undertook this work because we chose to, not because of external obligations. Our motivation was intrinsic, not extrinsic. Six years on, the strategies of Feedback for Learning are becoming the norm – the way our schools do business.

– Pauline Clarke
Superintendent of Schools—Inner City
The Winnipeg School Division

FURTHER READING

Assessment Reform Group. *Assessment for Learning: Beyond the Black Box.* Pamphlet. London, UK: The Author, 1999.

_____. *Testing Motivation and Learning / Assessment Reform Group.* Cambridge, UK: University of Cambridge Faculty of Education, 2002.

Berne, E. *Games People Play: The Basic Handbook of Transactional Analysis.* New York, NY: Ballantine Books, 1996.

Black, P., and D. Wiliam. "Inside the Black Box: Raising Standards Through Classroom Assessment." *Phi Delta Kappan* 80, No. 2 (October 1998): 139–144, 146–148.

Crooks, T.J. "The Impact of Classroom Evaluation Practices on Students." *Reviews of Educational Research* 58 (1988): 438–481.

Davies, A. *Making Classroom Assessment Work.* Courtenay, BC: Connections Publishing, 2000.

Davies, A., C. Cameron, C. Politano, and K. Gregory. *Together Is Better: Collaborative Assessment, Evaluation, and Reporting.* Winnipeg, MB: Portage & Main Press, 1992.

Egan, G. *Working the Shadow Side: A Guide to Positive Behind-the-Scenes Management.* San Francisco, CA: Jossey-Bass, 1994.

Gregory, K., C. Cameron, and A. Davies. *Knowing What Counts.* Vol. 1, *Setting and Using Criteria.* Courtenay, BC: Connections Publishing, 1997.

_____. *Knowing What Counts*. Vol. 2, *Self Assessment and Goal Setting*. Courtenay, BC: Connections Publishing, 2000.

_____. *Knowing What Counts*. Vol. 3, *Conferencing and Reporting*. Courtenay, BC: Connections Publishing, 2001.

Kolb, D.A. *Experience as the Source of Learning and Development*. Upper Saddle River, NJ: Prentice Hall, 1984.

Leahy, S., C. Lyon, M. Thompson, and D. Wiliam. "Classroom Assessment Minute by Minute, Day by Day." *Education Leadership*, ASCD 63, No. 3 (November 2005): 19–24.

O'Connor, K. *How to Grade for Learning. Linking Grades to Standards*. 2nd ed. Thousand Oaks, CA: Corwin Press, 2002.

Stiggins, R. *Classroom Assessment for Student Success*. Washington, DC: National Education Association, 1998.

Sutton, R. *School Self Review*. Salford, UK: RS Publications, 1994.

_____. *Assessment for Learning*. Salford, UK: RS Publications, 1995.

_____. *The Learning School*. Salford, UK: RS Publications, 1998.

Wiggins, G., and J. McTighe. *Understanding by Design*. 2nd ed. Alexandria, VA: Association for Supervision and Curriculum Development, 2005.